An ABC of Music

D0764676

Oxford
Paperback
Reference

The most authoritative and up-to-date reference books for both students and the general reader.

An ABC of Music

A short practical guide to the
basic essentials of rudiments,
harmony, and form

by IMOGEN HOLST

with a foreword by
BENJAMIN BRITTEN

Oxford   New York

OXFORD UNIVERSITY PRESS

Oxford University Press, Great Clarendon Street, Oxford OX2 6DP

Oxford New York
Athens Auckland Bangkok Bogota Bombay
Buenos Aires Calcutta Cape Town Dar es Salaam
Delhi Florence Hong Kong Istanbul Karachi
Kuala Lumpur Madras Madrid Melbourne
Mexico City Nairobi Paris Singapore
Taipei Tokyo Toronto

and associated companies
in Berlin Ibadan

Oxford is a trade mark of Oxford University Press

© *Oxford University Press 1963*

First published 1963
Reissued in new covers 1996

British Library Cataloguing in Publication Data

Data available

ISBN 0-19-317103-1

23 25 27 29 30 28 26 24

Printed in Great Britain by
Cox & Wyman Ltd, Reading, Berkshire

ACKNOWLEDGEMENTS

Acknowledgements are due to the following for permission to quote extracts from the works indicated:

G. Alsbach & Co. (Leo Editions Basart, Inc., Amsterdam): Sweelinck's *Werken voor Orgel en Clavicembal*, ed. Seiffert. Breitkopf & Härtel: *Altdeutsches Liederbuch*, ed. Böhme; John Bull's 'Alman' and 'Gigge', and 'Coranto' (anon.) from the *Fitzwilliam Virginal Book.* Harvard University Press: *Anthology of Music Vol. 1*, ed. A. Davison and W. Apel. Journal of Folk-Song Society, Nos. 9, 16, 19, 28 and 33. Macmillan & Co. Ltd.: Grove's *Dictionary of Music and Musicians* (article on Folk Music by Dr. O. M. Sandvik). Novello & Co. Ltd.: 'I'll go and enlist' (Morris tune, collected and edited by Cecil Sharp); *Folk Songs for Schools*, ed. Cecil Sharp. Oxford University Press: *English Folk Songs from the Southern Appalachians*, ed. Cecil Sharp; *New Oxford History of Music*, Vols. I and II. Royal Musical Association: T. Simpson's 'Ricercar' from Vol.9, *Musica Britannica.* Stainer & Bell Ltd.: R. Vaughan Williams's 'This is the truth' and 'Wassail Song'; Morley's 'Whither away so fast?', ed. Fellowes.

FOREWORD

A young friend of mine has been playing the guitar for several years now. He has a real aptitude for it : a feeling for the sound of the instrument, a considerable gift for technique, and patience to work hard. But he cannot read music and knows nothing of how music is made, and, what is more, he simply refuses to learn. 'Too dull and too much trouble', he says, 'and anyhow not worth it'. It is true, of course, that a lot of his time is spent in playing dance music, when sight-reading is perhaps not so essential, but he has a considerable interest in straight music, and the lute parts of Dowland have a real fascination for him. When this book is published I want to send him a copy, because he will see that learning to read music, and learning its grammar, need not be dull or too much trouble. He will also discover when he can sight-read that it is really 'worth it'. Maybe you *can* pick up tunes and approximate block harmonies without being able to read, but I challenge anyone with that (rather over-rated) gift of playing or singing 'by ear' to pick up easily and quickly a Dowland accompaniment *exactly* as he wrote it (and the 'exactly' matters), or the Stravinsky dance-rhythms, or the inner part of a complicated madrigal or part-song—as most of us with experience of amateur choral singing can testify.

No, it won't be only to this guitar boy that I shall send copies of this book, but to many of my friends who sing or play the recorder in amateur groups, and who spend frequent and distressing moments 'getting lost'.

Luckily most state and many private schools are now teaching rudiments of music as a matter of course. I strongly recommend teachers to use this book. Miss Holst has an unrivalled knowledge of teaching ; she knows how to keep

the interest of the pupil—by being serious, and yet not turgid ;
by being brief, but not telegrammic ; and by illuminating
her text with intelligent parallels from her wide knowledge
of art and life.

BENJAMIN BRITTEN

PREFACE

This book is a brief introduction to the language of music. Its purpose is to tell the reader how the basic sounds of the language can be recognized ; how they are written down ; how notes, with the help of rhythm, can become tunes ; how tunes can create harmony ; how harmony can lead to extended form, and how form is inseparable from the texture of music which can change with the changing needs of each century.

As its title suggests, this ABC begins at the very beginning and goes on step by step. It has been planned as a cumulative dictionary in which each definition leads to the next. No new technical term is used until a point has been reached where its definition becomes necessary. Each newly-defined word is set in capitals, and for readers who want to use the ABC as a reference book of rudiments there is an index of terms at the end. A fair number of facts will be familiar to a fair number of readers. Even beginners will find many things that they already know. But if they are hoping to learn the grammar of music thoroughly they would be well advised to read at any rate the first half of the book in the order in which it is written, and to try out the actual sound of each music example before going on to the next.

An ABC has to be brief : there is only room for plain statements of fact. Nor can any book take the place of a living teacher. Readers of the following chapters must not expect to learn how to harmonize, nor must they expect to be provided with a pocket history of music ; the short examples can only give a glimpse of some of the things that have happened in each century, and this roughly chronological order can only hint at the connecting thread that runs through the living language of music.

The language of music, like any other language, remains dead if it is confined to lists of rules in a text-book : a knowledge of French or German grammar is of little use unless it is going to lead in the end to conversation. The rules of musical grammar in the following chapters are intended for a wider use than text-book reference. They may, it is true, prove helpful to examination candidates who have not yet had a chance to ask ' Why ? ' But students are not the only readers I have had in mind. The book was also written for those amateur singers and players who still find sight-reading difficult, and for the increasing number of listeners who want to explore the sounds they are hearing. The aim of what follows is to encourage livelier singing or playing, and livelier listening.

I. H.

CONTENTS

xi

For Leonard and Dorothy Elmhirst

Part 1. The Musical Alphabet

CHAPTER 1

MUSICAL SOUNDS

SOUND is everything that we hear : a clock ticking, a door slamming, a dog barking, a car changing gear on the hill, the wind in the trees, a voice speaking in the next room and another voice singing in the house across the road.

A SINGING voice reaches further than a speaking voice. A muttered 'Where are you?' can be heard across a room, but if the question is to carry to the far end of a field the voice has to be pitched higher than in conversation and the spoken words have to be transformed into a call. Each word travels through the air on a long-drawn-out, unwavering level of sound :

                    ARE————
    ' Where————   you————?

The raising of the voice helps to bring out the meaning of the words, and the answering call may perhaps imitate, quite instinctively, the two different levels of sound :

                    ' COM————
                                ing !'

This is SINGING.

Each clear, sustained level of sound is a NOTE.

The height or depth of each note is its PITCH.

Changes in pitch can be measured as accurately as changes in temperature. The physical origin of a note is VIBRATION. (If you stretch an ordinary thin rubber band nearly as far as it will go and then twitch it with a finger or thumb, you can see the rapidly moving to-and-fro of the vibrations.)

It is the regular to-and-fro vibrations that produce MUSICAL

SOUNDS of a definite pitch.   Unmusical sounds are irregular and of indefinite pitch.

A vibration's complete to-and-fro is the unit for measuring changes in pitch.   The number of vibrations per second is called FREQUENCY.   A high note has a greater frequency than a low note.   The lowest note of a piano has an approximate frequency of 30 :   the highest note has a frequency of approximately 4000.

The two notes on ' COM———ing !' might possibly have the frequencies of 523 and 440, but no musician ever thinks about the actual number of vibrations in the notes he is singing.   He might begin by being ' given ' a note on an instrument, in order to get his bearings, but after that he would find the level of any other note in relation to the starting note. Some musicians, even when they are beginners, have what is called PERFECT PITCH :   they can immediately find the required level of sound for any note without any help. Others have to develop their powers of recognition until they can rely on their sense of RELATIVE PITCH.

Every musician, whether he is a composer, a singer, or an instrumentalist, has to train his mind's ear so that he can silently imagine the sound of any note, just as a painter in a darkened room can see in his mind's eye any colour of the spectrum.

The painter's choice of colours is wider than the musician's choice of notes, for the main colours of the spectrum can pass through so many gradual changes that they seem to merge into each other almost imperceptibly.   There are sounds such as the wind whistling in the chimney which move by infinitesimal degrees from one level of pitch to the next.   But these are uncontrollable sounds : they cannot be organized.   Musicians have to keep to a manageable number of levels for their notes. In the Far East music can move from one level to another through very small degrees called MICROTONES.   But in the West, composers limit themselves to a few definite levels of pitch.

A great deal of music is built on a working basis of only

SEVEN NOTES, with five ' extra ' notes held in readiness to be used when wanted.

The seven notes have the same names as the first seven letters of the alphabet : A, B, C, D, E, F, G. These are the ' white ' notes on the piano. (The piano is not essential in learning music, but it is helpful because all the notes are there all the time.) The ' black ' notes are the five ' extra ' notes for special occasions : their pattern of twos and threes makes it easy to recognize the position of the white notes :

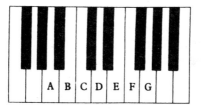

The pattern recurs over and over again. It is easiest to begin with the group of notes in the middle of the instrument, where the C is called MIDDLE C.

Heard one after another, these seven notes are like the steps of a ladder. They can be numbered : 1, 2, 3, 4, 5, 6, 7. The ladder sounds incomplete without the eighth step, which is called the OCTAVE. It is not a new note ; it is A, the same note as the first step, but instead of being at the bottom, it is now at the top of the completed ladder :

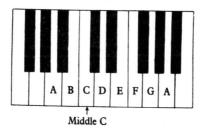

Middle C

The A above middle C is the note of a tuning-fork with frequency 440. This is the note orchestral players refer to in order to get IN TUNE before beginning to play. (Good INTONATION is singing or playing in tune ; bad intonation means ' out of tune '.)

The ladder of sound from A to its octave is called a SCALE.

A seven-note scale with its octave is often referred to as DIATONIC, from the Greek word for ' through the notes '.

The steps of a diatonic scale are not all the same size. The distance between B and C, and between E and F, is half the size of the other steps. Whole steps are called TONES : half-sized steps are SEMITONES.

The difference in sound between a tone and a semitone is vitally important in music. A good way to practise hearing the difference is to begin on the A above middle C and then sing or play a whole tone down to G, another whole tone down to F and a semitone down to E :

        A

          G

             F

               E

This pattern is called a TETRACHORD (from the four notes of a Greek stringed instrument.) The same pattern of two descending tones followed by a semitone can be begun on E, going down to B :

        E

          D

             C

               B

The ordinary letters of the alphabet are easy to follow in a pattern as simple as this, but in more elaborate music they would be confusing, so musicians have invented their own system of writing, called NOTATION.

CHAPTER 2

NOTATION

THE earliest written music that has survived in Europe is PLAINCHANT, or PLAINSONG. It is still used in Roman Catholic churches. Psalms and prayers are sung in prose with the rhythm and inflection of the spoken words.

The first medieval singers who wanted to write down their chants began by putting signs above the words to suggest the level of the notes. For an 'Amen' to the notes F—G they wrote the letter F as a clue where to start and then put a sign going up for the G :

Ex. 1

Ɣ • ✓
   A-men

It was in about the year 1000 that they thought of drawing a horizontal line coming out of the letter F to represent the level of sound at F. For the Amen in Ex. 1 they put a POINT on the line for F (that is, with the line going through it), and a point lying just above the line for G. (The points were square because of the quill pens they used.)

Ex. 1a

Ɣ—•——•—
    A- men

The letter F at the beginning of the line was called a CLEF, because it was a key, or clue, to the knowledge of the level of sound.

The letter C was also used as a clef. An 'Amen' beginning on C and going down to B would have been written :

Ex. 2

♭—•——▪—
   A -men

Later on, medieval musicians added three more horizontal lines to make it easier to write tunes that went further up or down. The four lines were called the STAFF or STAVE. The points representing ascending or descending notes of a scale were written alternately ON THE LINES or IN THE SPACES between the lines. The clef in those days could be written on any of the four lines. Although the lines of the stave were drawn an equal distance apart, the singers knew that *the distance in sound was not always equal*, for the position of the clef warned them of the semitones B—C or E—F:

Ex. 3

F E F G A G F E

Al - le - lu -ia, Al - le - lu - ia

This method of writing music is very nearly the same that we use today. We have added a fifth line to the stave. The points are now oval instead of square, and they are called NOTES, to represent the sound of the notes. (In America the word ' note ' is used only for the *written* note : the actual sound is called a ' tone '. American musicians say ' One sees a note and hears a tone ', but this does not apply in England.)

We still use the letter F for a clef : its shape has changed from) to 𝄢 . (Occasionally it is written ℮· ; but this version, which can be confusing, is almost obsolete.) In modern notation the F CLEF is always used with the dots on either side of the fourth line from the bottom of the stave, to represent the level of sound at F below middle C :

Ex. 3a

F E F G A G F E

The F clef is called the BASS CLEF. It is used for all low voices and instruments.

The C CLEF is not used so often in modern notation, but we still need it for several instruments with a medium range of pitch. The 𝄡 is now written 𝄡 and is centred either on the third line for the ALTO CLEF or on the fourth line for the TENOR CLEF. The line that it is centred on always represents the level of pitch at middle C :

Ex. 2a   Ex. 2b

Alto clef   C B   Tenor clef   C B

A - men   A - men

(same level of pitch as Ex. 2a)

A third clef was added in the sixteenth century. This is the G CLEF, which is now used for all higher voices and instruments. It is called the TREBLE CLEF, and it is written with a loop encircling the second line of the stave, to represent the level of pitch at the G above middle C. At first the G was written **G** or 𝄞. It has now become more ornamental :

Ex. 3b

F E F G A G F E

(sounding an octave higher than Ex. 3a)

Al - le - lu - ia, Al - le - lu - ia

In the descending tetrachord from E to B on page 4, the notes C and B, if written in the treble clef, need a temporary ' extra ' line of the stave, called a LEGER, or LEDGER LINE :

Ex. 4

E D C B

(The spelling ' leger ' is more usual, though ' ledger ' has the appropriate meaning of ' a horizontal timber in scaffolding '.)

Leger lines are used for any notes that are too high or too low for the stave. In Ex. 5 the white notes from the lowest C to the highest C of the piano are shown with the letter-names written in the way that is generally used when describing in words the level of pitch at each different octave. Middle C, referred to as *c'*, is shown in both clefs :

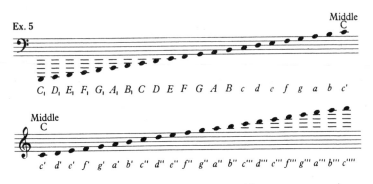

The lowest and highest notes in Ex. 5 have so many leger lines that they are difficult to recognize.   They are therefore written ALL' OTTAVA ('at the octave'), with the sign 8va . . . (or 8 . . .) as in Ex. 5A and Ex. 5B :

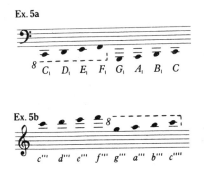

Ex. 5 has far too many notes to be learnt all at once.   The easiest way to recognize the look of them is to learn two or three at a time, repeating their names over and over again before going on to the next two or three.

Learning the MUSICAL ALPHABET is like learning the alphabet of any foreign language : the written syllables have to be practised as sound.   Isolated notes can never make musical sense, but as soon as they are related to each other in a tune, they become easy to remember.

CHAPTER 3

PHRASES

THE simplest tunes to begin practising are short PHRASES that move STEPWISE up and down, as in the plainsong Alleluias in Exs. 6, 7, and 8 :

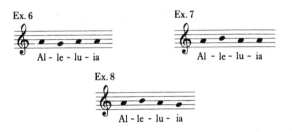

Each of these Alleluias has its own characteristic SHAPE. Although the steps are all a tone up or a tone down, the change of direction in the rise and fall makes it easy to distinguish one tune from another. In Ex. 9 the outline is the same as in Ex. 8, but the tune has a different character because the last two notes are only a semitone apart:

Ex. 9A is a VARIANT of Ex. 9 ; the third syllable has more than one note to it :

The curved line linking two notes in Ex. 9A is a SLUR. Notes that are slurred are always sung or played very smoothly and expressively, with a gentle stress at the beginning of the slur, and a gentle relaxation at the end of it :

In Ex. 11 the REPEATED NOTES at the beginning of the phrase are separated from each other by the consonant at the beginning of each new syllable, in contrast with the smooth rise and fall of the slurred notes :

In Ex. 12, the gap between the last two notes is called a LEAP. (But it can be sung just as smoothly as notes that move stepwise.) :

Stepwise phrases are described as being in CONJUNCT MOTION. Phrases with leaps are in DISJUNCT MOTION.

The distance in pitch between two notes is called a MELODIC INTERVAL.

A stepwise movement up or down is the melodic interval of a SECOND.

The leap at the end of Ex. 12, where the C and the A are three notes apart, is the melodic interval of a THIRD. (In reckoning the size of an interval, always begin on the *lower* note ; think of it as the first step of a stepwise ascent, and count ' one ' on it.) The third in Ex. 12 is described as a ' falling ' third, because of the direction of the leap.

In Ex. 13 the disjunct interval is a rising FOURTH :

Ex. 13

Al - le - lu - ia ___

(An easy way to practise intervals is to begin with filling in the gap by singing the missing stepwise notes : in Ex. 13, G A B C. Then leave out the notes that are not meant to be there, and the interval will look after itself.)

In Ex. 14 the melodic interval is a falling FIFTH :

Ex. 14

De - o gra - ti - as

The last two notes of Ex. 15 make the interval of a falling SIXTH :

Ex. 15

a ___ *etc.*

The rising interval between the second and third notes of Ex. 16 is a SEVENTH :

Ex. 16

e ___ *etc.*

The leap in Ex. 17 is the melodic interval of an OCTAVE :

Ex. 17

de -scen- dit de coe - lis. Et in - car - na -tus est *etc.*

The vertical strokes in Ex. 17 mark the end of a section of the chant. The phrase ' descendit de coelis ' is the end of a musical SENTENCE, and the phrase ' Et incarnatus est ' is the beginning

of another musical sentence.   Fragments of musical sentences
(and fragments of words, as in Exs. 15 and 16) may be useful
for recognizing melodic intervals, but we cannot get the whole
meaning of the music until we are given a whole musical
sentence, as in Ex. 18 :

Ex. 18

Al - le - lu   -   -   - ia,   Al - le - lu   -   -   - ia.

The COMMA above the stave in Ex. 18 is like a comma in a
sentence of words.   It shows the shape of the musical sentence
and allows the singer to take a new breath if necessary.

The sign above the last note in Ex. 18 is a PAUSE (sometimes
called a FERMATA).   It invites the singer to wait for longer
than usual on the note it is written over.

The approach to the final note in Ex. 18, where the D falls
to C, is called the CADENCE.   All the notes in a musical sentence
are travelling towards their cadence.

In the journey towards the cadence in Ex. 19, the notes are
GROUPED within the one long phrase :

Ex. 19

A   -   -   -   -   -   - men.

The grouping of the notes in Ex. 19 helps to express the
musical sense of the chant.   Expressive singing is like expressive speaking : notes, like words, have to be PHRASED in order
to make the meaning of the sentence clear.   When the
musical sentences in Exs. 18 and 19 are phrased, the arrival on
their final C feels like a home-coming.   Both tunes sound as
if they ' belong ' to C.   This sense of ownership makes C the
most important note in both Ex. 18 and Ex. 19.   Every tune
has its own most important note, which is called the TONIC.
(In plainsong it is called the ' Final '.)   The tonic is always
recognizable, in the same way that the subject of a spoken
sentence is always recognizable.   When we speak it is the

choice of words and the order in which they come that gives the subject its importance and the sentence its meaning. It is the same in the language of music : the choice of notes and the order in which they are used makes the tonic recognizable and gives the tune its musical meaning.

Chapter 4

MODAL SCALES

Any note can be chosen as a tonic. And each tonic can have its own scale. (Start on any white note on the piano and play stepwise up or down the white notes until you reach the octave of the note you began on.)

The 'white note' or 'natural' scales are called Modal Scales, from the word Mode, meaning 'manner'. Each modal scale has a name borrowed from ancient Greek modes. Our European modal scale starting on the tonic A is called Aeolian. Ex. 20 shows it ascending, and Ex 20a descending :

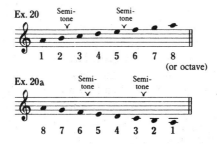

The figures below the notes in Exs. 20 and 20a show that each step or Degree of the scale is numbered in relation to the tonic. The numbers can be used for reckoning the melodic intervals from the tonic up to each scale degree : A to B is a second, A to C a third, A to D a fourth, A to E a fifth, A to F a sixth, A to G a seventh.

In the Aeolian scale the semitones between B and C and between E and F occur between the second and third degrees and between the fifth and sixth degrees of the scale.

In each modal scale the semitones are between different degrees, according to which note the scale has begun on. It is the position of the semitones in relation to the tonic that gives each mode its own particular character. (The following modal scales are given in an order that is easy to try out on the piano : in dictionaries modes are numbered according to their historical significance.)

MIXOLYDIAN :

Ex. 21

The tonic is G. The semitones are between the third and fourth and the sixth and seventh degrees.

LYDIAN :

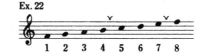

Ex. 22

The tonic is F. The semitones are between the fourth and fifth and the seventh and eighth degrees.

PHRYGIAN :

Ex. 23

The tonic is E. The semitones are between the first and second and the fifth and sixth degrees.

DORIAN :

Ex. 24

The tonic is D. The semitones are between the second and third and the sixth and seventh degrees.

IONIAN :

The tonic is C. The semitones are between the third and fourth and the seventh and eighth degrees.

The scale in Ex. 25 sounds more familiar than the others because a great deal of the music written during the last three hundred and fifty years has been founded on it. Tunes in this mode are no longer called Ionian : they are described as 'in C'. The Amen in Ex. 19 is in C. (We speak of tunes being founded on the notes of a scale, but this is not true of ancient music, for tunes came before scales, and many early tunes have fewer than seven notes in them.)

The Alleluia in Ex. 18 could be described as in C, but it could also be called PENTATONIC, because the sentence is founded on only five notes.

The word pentatonic can apply to a tune founded on any five notes : in Europe we use the name for gapped scales without semitones, for instance :

C D E G A C
D E G A C D
E G A C D E
G A C D E G
A C D E G A

In the modal scales on pages 13–15 there is no scale beginning on B. If you try playing a white-note scale on B you will find that the interval between the tonic and fifth is smaller than in the other modal scales. This makes B useless as a white-note tonic because the interval between the tonic and the fifth is the most important of all the intervals. Owing to its importance we call the fifth degree of any scale the DOMINANT. The to-and-fro between tonic and dominant can clearly be felt when singing a phrase such as the beginning of 'God rest you merry, Gentlemen' :

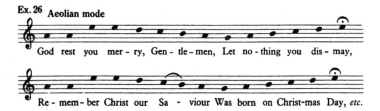

Ex. 26 Aeolian mode

God rest you mer – ry, Gen – tle – men, Let no – thing you dis – may,

Re - mem - ber Christ our Sa - viour Was born on Christ-mas Day, *etc.*

This magnetic pull between tonic and dominant is one of the many things that can help in keeping alive the RHYTHM of a tune.

Part 2.   Rhythm and Time

CHAPTER 5

PULSE AND TIME VALUES

ALL tunes have RHYTHM. Sometimes the rhythm is freely flowing, as in the plainsong ' Alleluia ' in Ex. 18. More often it is MEASURED, as in ' God rest you merry, Gentlemen ', with a regularly recurring PULSE. This pulse is not like the ticking of a clock : there is physical tension and relaxation in it. Any continuous action, such as walking, climbing, running, swimming, or rowing becomes easier as soon as it has this rhythmical give-and-take. (For instance, in walking upstairs, it is the relaxation on arriving at each step that provides new strength for the effort of going one higher.)

Unfortunately we often lose this effortless continuity when learning to ' keep TIME ' in music. The printed page appears to be bristling with unfamiliar difficulties : we stiffen in our anxious determination, and as a result our muscles become rigid and practically useless. But when the difficulties have been overcome, our limbs recover their normal activity and ' keeping time ' becomes as easy as walking or running. Music, by its very nature, has its own rhythm which can carry us along as soon as we stop struggling.

In the early stages of keeping time, a measured rhythm can be COUNTED, like the ' counting-out ' verses such as ' Eena, meena, mina, mo ', where each syllable is declaimed in a rhythmical pattern of ' longs ' and ' shorts ' :

Short	Short		Short	Short		Short	Short		LONG
Ee—na,			mee—na,			mi—na,			MO—

(The ' LONG ' is equal to two shorts, and the vertical strokes show that the pulse occurs at the beginning of each word.)

A rhythmical pattern in longs and shorts is called a TIME
PATTERN.   The time pattern of any song can be written above
its words in the musical notation for longs and shorts, as in
Ex. 27 :

Ex. 27 Good King Wen - ces - las look'd out

On   the   feast   of   Ste   -   phen,

When the snow lay round a - bout,

Deep and crisp and   e   -   ven,

Bright – ly shone the moon that night

Though the frost was cru   -   el,

When a poor man came in sight,

Gath – 'ring win – ter   fu - (oo) - el.———

The vertical strokes showing where the pulse occurs are
called BAR LINES.   The DURATION, or 'distance in time',
between one bar line and the next is a BAR.   (Americans call
a bar a MEASURE.)

The sign ♩ is called a CROTCHET.

The ♩ is a MINIM.

The ○ is a SEMIBREVE.

These signs ♩ , ♩ and ○ are TIME VALUES or NOTE VALUES.
They show how much the duration of a note is worth in

longs and shorts. The semibreve lasts as long as two minims or four crotchets. Americans use the words ' whole note ' for semibreve, ' half note ' for minim and ' quarter note ' for crotchet : they like to be reminded of the value of each note in relation to a semibreve.

Although the *pitch* of any note is fixed at a certain level, the *duration* of a note value can change from one tune to the next, according to the different SPEED of each tune. Words such as ' Quick ' or ' Slow ' are written at the beginning of a piece of music, to give some indication of the speed or TEMPO.

If a composer wants to give an exact indication of the tempo he has in mind, he shows how many crotchets or minims there would be in the duration of one whole minute. For instance, ♩ = 60 shows that it would take a minute for sixty crotchets to be sung or played. The second hand of a watch can be used for timing ♩ = 60 and for related speeds such as ♩ = 30 or ♩ = 120. A measured pendulum called a METRONOME gives the figure for any speed that is wanted. (Whatever the tempo may be, the proportions 𝅝 = ♩ ♩ = ♩ ♩ ♩ ♩ are always the same.)

CHAPTER 6

TIME PATTERNS IN CROTCHETS AND MINIMS

IN learning to keep time, the rhythm of a tune such as ' Good King Wenceslas ' can be counted according to the number of crotchets to the bar :

Ex. 27a

ONE	TWO	THREE	FOUR	ONE	TWO	THREE	FOUR
♩	♩	♩	♩	| ♩	♩	𝅗𝅥	
Good	King	Wen -	ces -	las	look'd	out_____	

It is unnecessary to write out the numbers in this way, as
there is a device called a TIME SIGNATURE which shows how to
count the time patterns in any bar.   A time signature consists
of two numbers, one on top of the other.   The lower number
represents the UNIT of time : it is written according to its
value in terms of a semibreve.   The unit in Ex. 27 is a crotchet,
so the lower figure of the time signature will be 4, because
four crotchets equal one semibreve.   (The American 'quarter
note' is helpful here.)   The number on the top of a time-
signature shows *how many units there are to the bar.*

In Ex. 27 there are four crochets to the bar, so the time
signature is $\frac{4}{4}$.

In combining time and pitch in written notes, the time
signature is written on the stave just before the first note of the
tune.   Crotchets and minims have their stems going upwards
on the right of the note when the pitch is below the middle
line of the stave, and downwards on the left for notes that are
above the middle line

Ex. 27b

The two vertical lines that are used at the end of every piece of music, or to show that a section has come to an end, are called a DOUBLE BAR. This is short for 'double bar-line'.

A conductor 'beating time' in Ex. 27B would show by his gestures—down, across, to the side, up—that the tune should be counted with four BEATS to the bar. When there is no conductor, the performers feel the beats for themselves. In all measured music, every singer or player is always instinctively aware of the beats in a bar, even though he may be far too experienced to have to count them.

A conductor, wanting his singers and players to begin together on the first note of Ex. 27B, would bring them in by giving them a silent PREPARATORY UP-BEAT, in the same speed as the tune. A preparatory beat is always felt as if it were part of the music. It is as necessary as a dancer's 'lift' before his first step.

The first beat of a bar is a MAIN PULSE or STRONG BEAT.

There is no need for an audible stress or ACCENT on the first beat of a bar unless the tune demands it. In the second bar of Ex. 27B, for instance, it would be inappropriate to have an accent on the weak syllable at the end of the name 'Wenceslas'. And in the last bar, an accent would destroy the smoothness of the long-drawn-out cadence. The strength of a strong beat is only made audible when the music itself asks for a stressed note.

The time signature for tunes with two crotchets to the bar is $\frac{2}{4}$, as in the folk-song in Ex. 28 :

Ex. 28
(Dorian mode)
Quick   German

The curved line linking the last two notes of Ex. 28 is a TIE (sometimes called a BIND). A tie joins two notes of the same pitch : it can never be confused with a slur, which links together notes of a different pitch. Tied notes always sound like one continuous note.

The time signature of a tune with three crotchets to the bar is $\frac{3}{4}$:

Ex. 29
(In C)
Moderately slow   German

CHAPTER 7

DOTTED NOTES AND QUAVERS IN SIMPLE AND COMPOUND TIME

If a $\frac{3}{4}$ tune needs a note lasting throughout the three beats, the two-beat minim is prolonged by putting a Dot after it. The dot shows that this particular minim must last for three crotchets instead of two:

Ex. 30
(Mixolydian)
Slow   German

Dotted notes are used in tunes with any number of beats to the bar, whenever a note has to last for one and a half times its normal length :

Ex. 31
(Aeolian)
Fairly quick   Polish

Whatever the time signature may be, *a dot after any note always makes it half as long again.*

Many tunes begin on the up-beat before the first main pulse. To balance this, the last bar is usually written with one beat missing.   This makes it possible to keep a continuous pulse if the tune is to be sung or played several times :

Ex. 32

The note that is half as long as a crotchet is a QUAVER. (In America, an 'eighth note', because there are eight quavers to a semibreve.)   A single quaver is written ♪ or ♮ (the tail is always to the right of the stem, whether the stem goes up or down.)   Two quavers together have their tails joined : ⌐ or ⌐ as in Ex. 33 :

Ex. 33

A dot after a crotchet makes it equal to three quavers (i.e. half as much again as its normal length) :

Ex. 34

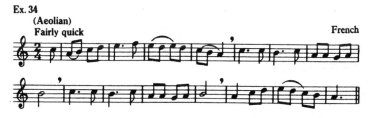

In Ex. 34 the first quaver comes half-way between the up-beat and the first main pulse.   Tunes can begin on any beat or

between any two beats of the bar.   The opening of Ex. 35
can be counted with a DIVIDED BEAT :   'and-three-and
one'.

Ex. 35

In Ex. 35 the quavers are GROUPED in this way to show where
each beat begins.   (But the first quaver's separate tail does not
interfere with the slur which links the three notes smoothly
together.)

In songs, it is usual to write each quaver with a separate
tail whenever the note has a word or a syllable to itself:

Ex. 36

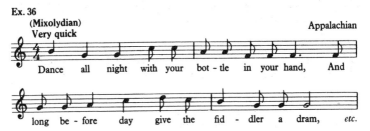

During the last few years several music publishers have broken
away from this tradition and we now find tails joined together
in the normal grouping of the time-pattern that is used when a
tune is to be played on an instrument :

Ex. 36a

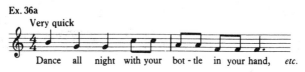

A quaver can be the unit of time in a tune ; it is represented
by the figure **8** in a time signature : $\frac{3}{8}$ $\frac{4}{8}$· $\frac{6}{8}$ $\frac{9}{8}$ etc.

$\frac{3}{8}$ is the time signature for tunes with three quavers to the bar. The beat in a $\frac{3}{8}$ tune need be no quicker than the beat in a $\frac{3}{4}$ tune : the speed, as always, will depend on the indication above the first bar :

Ex. 37

Tunes in $\frac{4}{8}$, with four quavers to the bar, are like tunes in $\frac{2}{4}$ with two crotchets to the bar, except that they are counted in quavers :

Ex. 38

$\frac{6}{8}$ is the time signature for tunes with six quavers to the bar. A bar of $\frac{6}{8}$ is like two bars of $\frac{3}{8}$ invisibly joined together. The grouping of the notes makes this clear :

Ex. 39

The six quavers to the bar in Ex. 39 are counted ' ONE two three FOUR five six '. (This is an entirely different rhythm from the three divided crotchets to the bar in Ex. 35, where the six quavers were counted ' ONE and Two and THREE and '.)

Very few $\frac{6}{8}$ tunes are slow enough to be counted in six quavers to the bar. Quick $\frac{6}{8}$ tunes are counted with a DOTTED-CROTCHET BEAT, in two beats to the bar. (Each beat has three quavers to it.):

Ex. 40

A $\frac{9}{8}$ bar is like three bars of $\frac{3}{8}$ joined together. Quick tunes are counted in three dotted-crotchet beats to the bar. (Each beat has three quavers to it.):

Ex. 41

There is no note that lasts for a whole bar of $\frac{9}{8}$, so a dotted minim is tied to a dotted crotchet to represent a continuous note with the value of three dotted crotchets : $\frac{9}{8}$ 𝅗𝅥.   𝅘𝅥. |

A $\frac{12}{8}$ bar is like four bars of $\frac{3}{8}$ or two bars of $\frac{6}{8}$. Tunes in $\frac{12}{8}$ are counted in four dotted-crotchet beats to the bar, with three quavers to the beat :

Ex. 42
(Dorian)
At a moderate speed: flowing   Swedish

Time signatures with a dotted-note beat are called COM-
POUND. In SIMPLE TIME the beat is divided into TWO. In
COMPOUND TIME the beat is divided into THREE.

CHAPTER 8

QUICK NOTES AND SLOW NOTES

THE note that is half as long as a quaver is a SEMIQUAVER. (In
America a ' sixteenth note '.) It is written 𝅘𝅥𝅯 or 𝅘𝅥𝅯 . Two or
more semiquavers have their tails joined:

𝅘𝅥𝅯𝅘𝅥𝅯 𝅘𝅥𝅯𝅘𝅥𝅯 𝅘𝅥𝅯𝅘𝅥𝅯𝅘𝅥𝅯𝅘𝅥𝅯 𝅘𝅥𝅯𝅘𝅥𝅯𝅘𝅥𝅯𝅘𝅥𝅯

When a tune contains quavers and semiquavers, the notes are
joined together in groups according to the time pattern, so
that each group shows where the new beat begins :

Ex. 43
(Dorian)
Quick and energetic   English

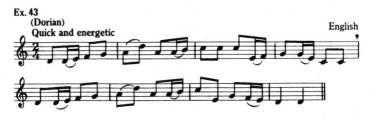

(The rule about stems going up for notes below the middle line
of the stave and down for notes on or above it cannot apply
when tails are joined together in a time pattern.)

The semiquaver is occasionally used as a unit in time
signatures, for example : $\frac{3}{16}$ $\frac{6}{16}$ $\frac{9}{16}$ $\frac{12}{16}$

A dot after a quaver makes it last for three semiquavers :

Ex. 44
(Aeolian)
Quick   English

etc.

A DOUBLE DOT after any note lengthens it by three quarters.
A doubly dotted crotchet is therefore equal to a crotchet plus
a quaver plus a semiquaver :

Ex. 45
(Dorian)
Slow   Hebridean

The note that is half as long as a semiquaver is a DEMISEMI-
QUAVER. (In America, a ' thirty-second note '.) It is written
♪ or ♩. Two or more are joined :

(The third horizontal line has nothing to do with three : it is
a symbol to show that the value of the semiquaver has been
halved.) A demisemiquaver is seldom found as a separate
note. It is usually grouped with semiquavers and quavers, as
in Ex. 46, where the time patterns can be counted in quavers—
' one-and-two-and '—during the early stages of learning the
tune :

Ex. 46
(Dorian)
Slow: very expressive   Irish

In Ex. 46 the notes are grouped, as is usual, according to the beats in the bar. Each complete $\frac{2}{4}$ bar has two groups, and each group is equal in length to a crotchet. But at the first beat in bars 2,3,4,5, and 7 the groups are SUBDIVIDED into quavers. This helps in reading time patterns with many notes to the crotchet, and it makes it easier to count ' one-and-two-and ' while learning the tune.

Demisemiquavers are not used in very quick music, for there would be no time to fit them in. Notes that look quick are often found in the slowest music. And tunes that consist of nothing but minims and crotchets often have a quick beat.

When a tune with four crotchets to the bar is sung or played very quickly, it becomes impossible to count or conduct four beats in a bar. The counting is therefore reckoned in minims instead of crotchets. There are two beats in a bar. The time signature is $\frac{2}{2}$. (The lower figure is 2 because there are two minims in a semibreve ; a minim is a ' half note '.)

Ex. 47

The time signature $\frac{3}{2}$ has three minims in a bar. It is counted in three beats to the bar :

Ex. 48
(Dorian)
At a moderate speed   English

Very slow $\frac{3}{2}$ tunes can be counted with a divided beat, as in Ex. 49 :

Ex. 49
(Aeolian)
Slow: quietly flowing   Manx
    and THREE and   ONE and TWO and THREE and   ONE

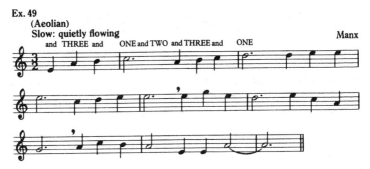

The rhythm of Ex. 49 is quite different from the rhythm of Ex. 50, where the time signature is $\frac{6}{4}$. A bar of $\frac{6}{4}$ is like two bars of $\frac{3}{4}$ joined together. The beat is a dotted minim, and there are two beats to the bar :

Ex. 50
(Phrygian)
At a moderate speed   English
    ONE   TWO   ONE   TWO

(Exs. 49 and 50 show the difference between simple and compound time.)

The time signature $\frac{6}{4}$ is mostly found in old music, where it is the equivalent of our modern $\frac{6}{8}$.

The compound time signatures $\frac{9}{4}$ and $\frac{12}{4}$ are sometimes found in old music : they are the equivalent of our modern $\frac{9}{8}$ and $\frac{12}{8}$.

Another time signature that is mostly found in early music is $\frac{4}{2}$, with four minim-beats to the bar. It is sometimes used for hymns.

In ⁴₂ the note that lasts for a whole bar is a BREVE. It is
written ◻ or ◻ :

Ex. 51

(The name ' breve ' is a legacy from medieval times when it
was a ' short ' note : a minim was then the ' least ' note of all.
A long note was called *longa*, and the longest note of all was
a *maxima*.)

CHAPTER 9

RESTS

MUSIC consists of silences as well as sounds.   These silences are
called RESTS.   Every note has an equivalent rest which lasts
the same length of time and shares the same name in time
values :

Breve rest	
Semibreve rest	(⬮ when shown without a stave)
Minim rest	(⬮ when shown without a stave)
Crotchet rest	
Quaver rest	
Semiquaver rest	
Demisemiquaver rest	

(In old-fashioned editions of music the crotchet rest is sometimes written ⌐ like a quaver rest facing the wrong way.
This sign is seldom used today.)

Rests are often used as BREATHING-PLACES in a tune :

Ex. 52
(Pentatonic)
Fairly slow   Chinese

Rests are just as important as notes.   Their silences are
never static.   They belong to the rhythm of the tune, and the
continuous pulse of the music can be felt through them :

Ex. 53
(In C)
Lilting (two in a bar)   Scottish

I won - der when I'm to be mar - ried,
mar - ried, mar - ried, I won - der when I'm to be
mar - ried be - fore my beau - ty de - cays.

(The rests in Ex. 53 are grouped in this way because of the division of the $\frac{6}{8}$ bar into two beats with three quavers to a beat.)

As a general rule, a separate rest is used for each silent beat of a bar. For example :

If a $\frac{4}{4}$ tune has a half-bar of silence either at the beginning or the end of the bar, the silence is written as a minim rest instead of two crotchet rests :

Ex. 54

etc.

In tunes in compound time, a silent beat may be written either as a dotted rest, or as two rests :

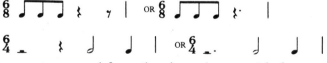

(If two rests are used for a silent beat, the rest with the greater value always comes first.)

Whatever the time signature may be, a SILENT BAR is always written with a semibreve rest. This semibreve rest is a symbol representing a silence lasting for as many beats as are shown in the time signature. (In $\frac{4}{2}$ a breve rest can be used, though this is becoming obsolete.)

CHAPTER 10

REPEATS

IN writing music, one of the most useful of all labour-saving devices is the REPEAT SIGN. This is written as a double bar with a dot above and below the middle line of the stave :  When the dots are on the left of the double bar they mean ' Go back from here and do that section again '. In Ex. 37 (page 25) where bars 5—8 are an exact repetition of bars 1—4, the repeat sign could be used :

Ex. 37a
Slow

Two dots to the right of a double bar mean ' This is where you go back to.' In Ex. 34 (page 23), where bars 9—12 are an exact repetition of bars 5—8, repeat signs could be used, as in Ex. 34A :

Ex. 34a
Fairly quick

Many tunes have a section that is repeated with exactly the same notes until the last few bars. Ordinary repeat signs are used with ⌐1 ⌐ and ⌐2 ⌐ to show that at the end of the repeated section the passage marked ⌐1 ⌐ is to be left out and the passage marked ⌐2 ⌐ is to be sung or played instead of it. Ex. 43 could be written with these signs for FIRST TIME and SECOND TIME bars :

Ex. 43a

If the repeated sections of a tune begin on an up-beat, the double bar of the repeat sign will cut into the last bar of each section and make it look incomplete, but the time pattern will always be balanced by the up-beat :

Ex. 55

In Ex. 55 the last section is an exact repetition of the first section. There is no need to write it out all over again. At the end of the second section we can use the words DA CAPO AL FINE, meaning ' Go back to the beginning and repeat the music until you get to the Italian word FINE, meaning " end ".' :

Ex. 55a

The words DAL SEGNO AL FINE show that instead of going back to the beginning, the player or singer should go back to whatever bar is marked with the sign 𝄋.

CHAPTER 11

SUMMARY OF TIME SIGNATURES

IN the early stages of learning the language of music it is helpful to memorize the rules of grammar, just as in learning a foreign language it is necessary to memorize the conjugation of verbs and the declension of nouns.   Time signatures are listed under the names DUPLE, TRIPLE and QUADRUPLE, according to whether there are two, three, or four beats to the bar.

SIMPLE DUPLE:	$\frac{2}{2}$	$\frac{2}{4}$	$\frac{2}{8}$
SIMPLE TRIPLE:	$\frac{3}{2}$	$\frac{3}{4}$	$\frac{3}{8}$
SIMPLE QUADRUPLE:	$\frac{4}{2}$	$\frac{4}{4}$	$\frac{4}{8}$
COMPOUND DUPLE:	$\frac{6}{4}$	$\frac{6}{8}$	$\frac{6}{16}$
COMPOUND TRIPLE:	$\frac{9}{4}$	$\frac{9}{8}$	$\frac{9}{16}$
COMPOUND QUADRUPLE:	$\frac{12}{4}$	$\frac{12}{8}$	$\frac{12}{16}$

Whatever the time signature may be, the written notes are grouped together so that each group is equal in value to one beat. There are several exceptional groupings.

In ⁴⁄₄, if half the bar consists of nothing but quavers, they are grouped together :

In ²⁄₄ and ³⁄₄ a whole bar of quavers is grouped together :

In ³⁄₈ a whole bar of quavers or of semiquavers is grouped together :

⁴⁄₄ is sometimes referred to as COMMON TIME. In some early editions of music, C is written instead of ⁴⁄₄. This C does not stand for ' common ' : it is meant to be a half-circle, which is a relic of the medieval system of notation.

¢ is another legacy from the Middle Ages. It represents ²⁄₂, and is found only in old editions. ²⁄₂ is sometimes called ALLA BREVE, but the name is not helpful, as it was originally used for four semibreves to the bar. These occasional inconsistencies are the result of having adapted an earlier system to suit very different needs. Our present system of notation works well on the whole, and we have to be grateful that anything as subtle as rhythm can be indicated in written time patterns.

CHAPTER 12

LESS FAMILIAR TIME PATTERNS

THERE are several time signatures that do not fit into the text-book categories of duple, triple, and quadruple. These include QUINTUPLE time signatures ($\frac{5}{2}$, $\frac{5}{4}$, $\frac{5}{8}$, $\frac{5}{16}$). In many quintuple tunes the five can be felt as $2+3$ or $3+2$. Numbers in brackets are sometimes written over the bars to show whether they are to be counted ' one two THREE four five ' or ' one two three FOUR five ' :

Ex. 56
(Aeolian)
Fairly slow   English

This   is   the   truth —   sent   from a - bove,   The

truth   of   God, —   the   God   of   love,   *etc.*

In SEPTUPLE time signatures ($\frac{7}{2}$, $\frac{7}{4}$, $\frac{7}{8}$, $\frac{7}{16}$) the bar can often be counted as $3+4$ or $4+3$. DOTTED BAR LINES are sometimes used to show these groupings :

Ex. 57
(In C)
Slow   Scottish

Any number of units can be written in a bar, provided the number is not too large to be manageable. Whatever the number, it will always be possible to divide it into groups of TWOS or of THREES or of a mixture of TWOS AND THREES. For instance, $\frac{11}{8}$ could be counted as $2+2+2+2+3$, or as $3+3+2+3$, and so on.

In simple time a beat *can* if necessary be divided into three instead of two. This exceptional time pattern is called a TRIPLET. The notes of a triplet are quicker than usual, as there are three of them to be fitted into the same length of time as the normal two. A triplet is written with a figure 3 above it:

Ex. 58
(Dorian)
Fairly slow   English

A triplet can consist of notes and rests, or of notes of different values. A square bracket is used to link them :

Tunes in compound time sometimes have a beat divided into two instead of three. This exceptional time pattern is called a DUPLET. A figure 2 is written above the notes, which are slower than usual, as there are only two of them to be fitted into the same length of time as the normal three :

Ex. 59

(Pentatonic)
Quick   Australian (aboriginal)

CHANGES OF TIME SIGNATURE can occur anywhere in a tune. If the change is from simple to compound, or compound to simple, it is necessary to show how the different speeds of the note values are related :

Ex. 60

(Aeolian)
Fairly quick   English

An alternative way of showing the relationship in Ex. 60 is to write it as follows :

Time patterns can get an exciting new lease of life by allowing their notes to arrive unexpectedly off the beat :

This arrival *between* the beats of the bar is called SYNCOPATION. A short note followed by a long note is an essential characteristic of syncopated tunes.   The Greek word means ' shortening by cutting '.

Other unexpected time patterns include CROSS-RHYTHMS, which disregard their bar-lines and enjoy a temporary new rhythm of their own, as in the second half of Ex. 62 :

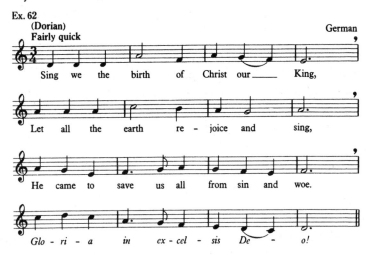

The tune follows the spoken rhythm of the words, so that at ' save us *all* from *sin* ' the two bars of $\frac{3}{4}$ are phrased as if they had turned into one bar of $\frac{3}{2}$. And the same thing happens at ' in excelsis Deo '. (This particular kind of cross-rhythm is called HEMIOLIA; a Greek word implying the ratio 3 : 2.)

Some tunes are meant to be sung or played very freely, without any regular pulse. They are written without any time signature or bar-lines. The word ' freely ', which is used to describe Ex. 63, can be written AD LIBITUM (or AD LIB.) meaning ' at will '. It can also be written as SENZA MISURA, meaning ' without the measurement of a bar with a time signature ':

Ex. 63

(Aeolian)
Freely   Norwegian

The written notes of any tune, whether measured or unmeasured, can only provide a bare statement of facts. Music cannot come to life until it is phrased rhythmically, and RHYTHM depends on much more than time patterns and speeds and correct breathing-places. It depends, among other things, on ' expression ', which varies with the shape and character of each tune, and with the louds and softs that occur in it. Expression cannot be taught : it has to be felt through all the subtle changes of tension and relaxation that are continually happening in music.

Part III.   Tension and Relaxation

CHAPTER 13

EXPRESSION MARKS AND DYNAMICS

THE pulse of measured music is never rigid like a machine. It is more like the pulse of a human being, for it can vary its speed without losing its life-giving momentum.   Tunes often slow down before coming to rest.   This slight slowing down is indicated by the word RALL. (short for RALLENTANDO) or by the word RIT., meaning either RITARDANDO (retarding) or RITENUTO (holding back).

A *rall.* or *rit.* is not only used at the end of a piece of music. If it is needed elsewhere, a dotted line is written after the word to show how long the slowing down is to last.   When the music returns to its normal speed the words A TEMPO are written above the stave.   (' Tempo ' in music means ' speed ' rather than ' time '.)

If the pulse of a piece of music is to become gradually quicker the word ACCEL. (short for ACCELERANDO) is used.* A dotted line shows how long the acceleration is to last, and *A tempo*, or *Tempo* 1°, meaning ' primo ', is written when the pulse returns to its original speed.

Every tune has its own character.   In a song, the words tell us what that character is, but in instrumental music the player often needs the help of EXPRESSION MARKS.   Slurs show the phrasing at a glance, but separate-looking minims and crotchets may also be intended to be played smoothly.   The

---

* The pronunciation of the Italian terms used in this book is shown in the index.

word LEGATO, meaning 'smooth', tells the player what is wanted.

Quick, energetic tunes often need to have every note played separately. The word STACCATO (or STACC.), meaning 'detached', shows that each note is to be brought off short. If a tune has a mixture of slurred notes and staccato notes, the staccato notes are written with a dot above or below them. (Staccato notes must never be called 'dotted notes', as it would lead to confusion with the notes that are lengthened in value by having a dot placed *after* them.)

If a tune has some staccato notes and also some unslurred notes which are meant to be held throughout their whole length, the sustained notes can be written with a short line over them :

(The short line is sometimes called TENUTO, from the verb 'to hold'. This word 'tenuto', often written *ten.*, can be used to warn the singer or player not to leave a note too soon.)

Detached notes that are not light and prickly enough to be called staccato are described as SEMI-STACCATO. They can be written with a slur or a line over their staccato dots :

Staccato notes that are to be played with marked energy and brought off very abruptly have vertical DASHES instead of dots over them :

(Any note-values can be staccato, but long notes such as minims are usually semi-staccato, unless the tempo is very quick. And a group of short notes, such as semiquavers, can only be staccato if the speed is slow enough to allow each note to be detached.)

An ACCENT, shown by the sign >, brings extra stress to a note :

A held note that is to be accented is often written *sf.* This is short for SFORZANDO, meaning ' reinforced '. *Sf.* implies that a long note will be louder at the beginning than at the end.

The gradations of loudness and softness in music are called DYNAMICS.

Loudness can be accurately measured. The vibrations that give us the frequency of a note also tell us about its loudness. The distance to-and-fro that a vibrating surface moves from its position of rest is called its AMPLITUDE. The greater the amount of energy used to produce a vibration, the greater its amplitude will be, and the louder the sound.

Fortunately for musicians, the amplitude of vibrations has no effect on the frequency of the note. This is one of the miracles of ACOUSTICS, or the science of sound.

Loudness is measured in units called DECIBELS, of which 1 represents the quietest sound the human ear can hear. A single decibel only just crosses what is known as the ' threshold of sound '. A whisper measures 10—20 decibels : a pneumatic drill equals 110 ; and any sound above 130 decibels, such as the noise of a jet plane, approaches—or even crosses—the ' threshold of pain '.

Musicians never reckon in decibels.* They think of their louds and softs as relative, using the word FORTE, written *f*, for loud, and PIANO, written *p*, for soft. Other dynamics are :

ff	=	fortissimo	=	very loud
pp	=	pianissimo	=	very soft
mf	=	mezzo forte	=	half loud
mp	=	mezzo piano	=	half soft (that is, between *mf* and *p*).

* Except in electronic music.

On special occasions, *fff* and *ppp* (or even *pppp*) can be written, but these extremes are rarely used.

If a piece of music is to become gradually louder, the word CRESCENDO, or CRESC., is written, meaning ' growing ' or ' increasing in loudness '. Gradually getting softer is indicated by the word DIMINUENDO, or DIM., meaning ' waning ', or ' decreasing in loudness '. *Cresc.* and *dim.* are not only continuous : they are accumulative. At the end of a *cresc.* or *dim.* a new dynamic is needed, to show what degree of loudness or softness has been reached.

A short *cresc.* is usually indicated by the sign ——◁ and a short *dim.* by the sign ▷—— .

High notes, owing to their greater frequency, have more tension than low notes. But it would be a mistake to crescendo on every rising phrase and diminuendo on every falling phrase. Expression in music is much more subtle than that. Every tune has its own balance of tension and relaxation. One of the easiest ways of recognizing this balance is to hear what happens to a tune when it is no longer sung or played on its own, but has other notes sounding together with it.

CHAPTER 14

INTERVALS

WHEN two different notes are sung or played together the listener can hear them simultaneously, as clearly as if they were sounding one after the other. Heard together, the two sounds blend into one, but without losing their own identity. The combined sound is called an INTERVAL.

Intervals are known by the same names as the melodic intervals in Chapter 3 and, like them, they are reckoned from the lowest note, which is called 1. For example :

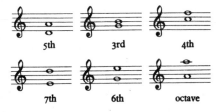

The interval of a second cannot be written with one note immediately above the other, as there is not enough room on the stave.   Therefore the higher note is written to the right of the lower note :

When the same note is sung or played simultaneously by more than one voice or instrument, the sound is described as a UNISON.

Semibreves in unison are written  or

Other note values in unison share the same head to the note but are given two stems, one going up and the other coming down :

(The rule on page 20 about stems going up for notes below the middle line of the stave and down for notes above it only applies to a single line of melody.)

Intervals can be built on any note of any scale.   The actual size of the interval, measured in tones and semitones, varies according to the position of the semitones in the scale.   For instance, D to E is a second, and E to F is a second, but D—E is the larger second because its two notes are a whole tone apart, whereas the distance between E and F is only a semitone. D—E is therefore called a MAJOR SECOND, while E—F is a MINOR SECOND. In the 'white-note' or 'natural' modal scales on pages 13-15, the only other minor second is B—C. All the remaining seconds are major.

By a process of listening-and-reckoning one can discover that the white-note thirds measure either two whole tones, as in the MAJOR THIRDS C—E, F—A, G—B, or a tone and a half, as in the MINOR THIRDS A—C, B—D, D—F and E—G.

White-note fourths, with one exception, all measure two and a half tones. They are called PERFECT FOURTHS. The exception is the fourth from F up to B, where the two notes are three tones apart. This uncomfortable interval, often referred to as the TRITONE, is an AUGMENTED FOURTH because it is a semitone too large.

All the fifths in the modal scales are PERFECT FIFTHS, measuring three and a half tones, except the fifth from B up to F which is a semitone too small and is therefore called a DIMINISHED FIFTH. The intervals B—F and F—B are actually the same size, because the distance between the notes of each interval adds up to three whole tones. But from B up to F is a fifth and from F up to B is a fourth, because *intervals are always reckoned by counting up from one letter-name to the other.*

Sixths are major if they measure four and a half tones and minor if they measure four tones. The difference in sound between a major and a minor sixth becomes easy to recognize if the upper note of the interval is moved down by step to a perfect fifth : if the sixth is a tone higher than the perfect fifth it is a MAJOR SIXTH ; if it is a semitone higher it is a MINOR SIXTH.

C—A, D—B, F—D, G—E are major sixths.

A—F, B—G, E—C are minor sixths.

Sevenths are major if they measure five and a half tones : minor if they measure five tones. The difference in sound between a major and a minor seventh can easily be recognised when the upper note of the interval is moved up by step to

an octave : if the seventh is a semitone below the octave it is
a MAJOR SEVENTH ; if it is a tone below the octave it is a
MINOR SEVENTH.

C—B and F—E are major sevenths.

A—G, B—A, D—C, E—D and G—F are minor sevenths.

Intervals that are more than an octave apart are COMPOUND
INTERVALS.   They are described in the same way as if they were
within the octave ; for instance :

compound 6th   compound 4th

Compound seconds and thirds
are usually called NINTHS and
TENTHS :

9th   10th

Intervals can be turned upside-down, or INVERTED, by
moving the lower note up an octave so that it becomes the
upper note.

An inverted unison becomes an octave:

An inverted second becomes a seventh:

An inverted third becomes a sixth:

An inverted fourth becomes a fifth:

An inverted fifth becomes a fourth:

An inverted sixth becomes a third:

An inverted seventh becomes a second:

An inverted octave becomes a unison:

Major intervals, when inverted, become minor.
Minor intervals, when inverted, become major.
Augmented intervals, when inverted, become diminished.
Diminished intervals, when inverted, become augmented.
Perfect intervals, when inverted, remain perfect.

CHAPTER 15

CONSONANCE AND DISSONANCE

WHEN different intervals are tried out on the piano, the ear welcomes some of them while finding others less pleasing. If the piano has been well tuned, the interval of the octave will sound thoroughly agreeable and satisfied and CONSONANT, while the interval of the major seventh, from F to E or C to B, cannot help sounding disagreeable and dissatisfied and DISSONANT.

The decision as to whether an interval is a CONSONANCE or a DISSONANCE is not just a matter of personal likes or dislikes : it is a matter of what happens to the sound vibrations when two notes are heard at once. Each note of an interval has its own frequency : for example, the note *a'* has a sound-wave of 440 vibrations per second, and the note *c"* has a sound-wave of 523. The waves are real waves : they rise to a crest and sink to a trough. When *a'* and *c"* sound together, their crests and troughs do not coincide. The two pathways cross and recross, meeting at different points on their separate journeys. These meeting-places set up a kind of knocking, faint but persistent, which sounds slightly restless and uncomfortable. The knocking varies with each interval, and it can be accurately measured, because wave-lengths are mathematically reliable. The graph of dissonance shows that the tension of discomfort is at its greatest in the intervals of the minor second and the major seventh.   The major second and the minor seventh are still dissonant, but they are not quite so piercingly uncomfortable.   The tritone is also tense, and there is a slight knocking, or BEATING, in major and minor thirds and sixths.   But there is hardly any disturbance in the perfect fourth, the perfect fifth and the octave.   The unison, with its sound-waves coinciding, is utterly at rest.

The accurate measurements on the graph of dissonance make it possible to describe intervals as belonging to three different categories :   perfect consonances, imperfect consonances, and dissonances.

Unisons, octaves, perfect fifths and perfect fourths are PERFECT CONSONANCES.

Major thirds, minor thirds, major sixths and minor sixths are IMPERFECT CONSONANCES.   Their slightly uncomfortable ' beating ' prevents them from being included with the perfect consonances, but it is not disagreeable enough for them to be described as dissonances.

Major seconds, minor seconds, major sevenths, minor sevenths and augmented and diminished intervals are DISSONANCES.

Consonant intervals sound satisfied, and can be at rest. Dissonant intervals are tense, and sound as if they were longing to move somewhere else to escape from their discomfort. Music needs dissonance as well as consonance, for it is the alternation between tension and relaxation that keeps it alive.

Part IV.   Counterpoint

CHAPTER 16

THE BEGINNINGS OF COUNTERPOINT

THE earliest medieval experimenters kept to perfect consonances when they first tried singing in intervals.   They gave the principal voice a familiar bit of plainsong at its normal pitch, while a second voice sang the same tune a fifth lower (Ex. 64) or a fourth lower (Ex. 65):

Ex. 64   9th century

Sit   glo – ri – a   Do – mi – ni,   in   sae – cu – la   *etc.*

Ex. 65

nunc   et   us – que   in   sae – cu – lum__

The two voices in Exs. 64 and 65 are described as being in PARALLEL MOTION because they keep the same distance apart when rising and falling.

In this primitive kind of part-singing ninth-century musicians found that parallel motion was easy except when they had to sing a fourth above F or a fifth above B.   Whenever this happened, the tritone came as an uncomfortable shock.   In order to avoid this discomfort, the singers moved B down a

semitone whenever it had to be sung with an F.   This process
of lowering a note for the distance of a semitone is called
FLATTENING.

The sign for a FLAT is ♭.   It is written just before the note,
on the appropriate line or space :

Al – le – lu – ia   A – men

(Today we can flatten any of the seven notes whenever we want
to ; but in the early Middle Ages B♭ was the only flattened
note.)

In Exs. 66 and 67 the B♭ helped the medieval singers to
avoid the tritone, but it meant going outside the chosen mode,
and in their efforts to keep within the mode they sometimes
began singing on a unison and then moved outwards to a
fourth or fifth, returning to a unison at the end of a phrase:

Ex. 68   9th century

Rex coe – li Do – mi – ne mar – is un – di – so – ni   Te hu – mi –
Ti – ta – nis ni – ti – di squa – li – di – que so – li,   Se ju – be –

– les   fa – mu – li   mo – du – lis   ve – ne – ran – do   pi – is
– as   fla – gi – tant va – ri – is   li – be – ra – re   ma – lis.

In Ex. 68 the voices are no longer confined to parallel motion,
and they are able to sing other intervals than perfect consonances.   At the beginning of each section of the hymn they
pass through the dissonance of a second and the imperfect
consonance of a third.   Yet there is no shock of discomfort,
and the dissonant interval is easy to sing.   This is because the
tune is conjunct : the dissonant second is approached and left
by step, while the lower voice remains safely anchored at the

same level of pitch. The method of writing for two voices when one stays on the same note and the other moves up or down is described as OBLIQUE MOTION.

At the end of each section of Ex. 68 one voice moves up while the other moves down. This movement in opposite directions is called CONTRARY MOTION. Its discovery had an exciting effect on the art of ' note-against-note ', or COUNTER-POINT. From then onwards, for the next six hundred years, voices became more and more independent, and each voice had a tune of its own, as in Ex. 69, where the lower voice sings the notes of the original plainsong, called the CANTUS, while the upper voice sings an independent tune called the DISCANTUS, or DESCANT :

By the beginning of the twelfth century musicians had discovered that voices could be independent in rhythm. Instead of keeping to note-against-note in their counterpoint, the principal voice sang a cantus in slow, long-drawn-out notes, with each note approximately the same length, while the upper voice sang a descant in quicker notes :

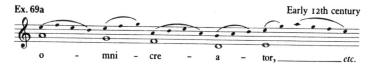

The drawing out of the tune into long, slow notes is called AUGMENTATION.

Soon after this the rhythm of church music became measured. In Ex. 70 the lower voice sings a plainsong tune in slow notes of exactly equal length while the upper voice

sings its own version of the tune in a rhythmical time pattern
of quicker notes :

Ex. 70   Late 12th century

Do

etc.

In Ex. 70A, which is founded on the same plainsong as
Ex. 70, the principal voice is freed from the restriction of
keeping to one note to a bar, and moves with a more enter-
prising rhythm, while the two voices show their greater
independence by changing places, or CROSSING PARTS, in the
fifth bar :

Ex. 70a   13th century

Do – mi – no   fi – de – li – um⏜o – mni – um

Do –   –   –   –   –   –   –   etc.

The dissonance on the main pulse at the beginning of the
fourth bar in Ex. 70A adds to the liveliness of the music.   The
reason it is easy to sing is because it is approached by step in
contrary motion.   (This is true of all the dissonant intervals
that have been written ever since.   Nothing is impossible to
sing if it is in smooth contrary motion.)

   The crossing-over of voices led to an exciting new development in counterpoint.   Singers borrowed phrases from each
other, one voice singing the same notes that the other had been
singing a few notes earlier, as in Ex. 71.   (The voices are
written on separate staves joined by a bracket, or BRACE.   This
is to avoid the cluttered-up appearance of crossed parts sharing
a stave.   The eye soon gets used to reading two staves at once.)

Ex. 71

13th century

The ' borrowing of phrases ', called IMITATION, was responsible for the epoch-making discovery that it is possible for several voices to sing exactly the same tune, beginning one after another, as in *Sumer is icumen in*, which is called a ROUND because the tune comes over and over again like the the turning of a wheel :

Ex. 72

Anon. 13th century

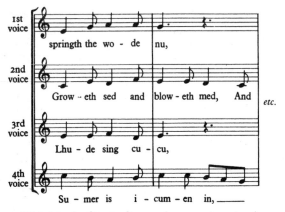

This kind of imitation, where each voice keeps strictly to the same tune, is called CANON, from the Greek word for keeping a thing straight and regulating it. (The words ROUND and CANON are sometimes used as if they were interchangeable, but there is a difference between them : in a round, the second voice enters when the first voice has got to the end of a phrase in the words, but in a canon the second voice can enter when the first voice is still in the middle of a word.)

Voices in canon need not follow each other at the same level of pitch : one voice often enters a fourth lower or a fifth higher than the other, as in Ex. 73 :

Ex. 73

Writing in canon is one of the most exciting of all the ways in which a composer can combine sounds. It introduces a new dimension in music, for the listener is anticipating as well as remembering what he hears.

The invention of canon helped to bring about the ' Golden Age ' of sixteenth-century contrapuntal or POLYPHONIC music (that is, ' many-sounding ', or, more accurately, ' many-voiced ' music).

Throughout Europe there were so many great composers writing music that it would take a long life-time to become familiar with even a small proportion of their works. In England alone there were so many masterpieces written that no twentieth-century English choir could ever complain of exhausting the possibilities of finding a work for a concert.

The original sixteenth-century part-books in the British Museum and other collections need a scholar to read them, as time-signatures and key-signatures were written differently four hundred years ago. Recently many practical editions have been published, so that present-day amateurs are able to sing polyphonic music.

Students of counterpoint try to learn from sixteenth-century composers by getting to know their music, in the same way that students of literature read the greatest writers in order to learn the grammar of a language from living works of art.

CHAPTER 17

RENAISSANCE COUNTERPOINT

LEARNERS often think of counterpoint as a series of struggles to fit the various voice parts together without breaking any of the rules. But the Renaissance composers of the sixteenth century enjoyed keeping within their chosen limitations, and they never allowed the intricate interweaving of the counterpoint to damage the satisfying MELODIC LINE of the music.

Their melodic lines often grew out of the gesture of the words, as in the rising phrase for ' ascendit ' in Ex. 74 :

This kind of word-painting for ' high ' or ' low ' never involved the singers in notes that were uncomfortably high or low for their voices, for composers kept to a limited range or COMPASS of notes for each voice part, choosing the level that suited each individual singer.

The distribution of the melodic lines among the different voices, each singing a fourth or fifth higher or lower than the next, led to an adjustment in contrapuntal imitation. An answering voice, imitating in canon a fourth lower, was not always able to imitate the phrase in exactly the same shape, because the to-and-fro relation of tonic-to-dominant was so compelling that it had to be answered by dominant-to-tonic, as in Ex. 75 :

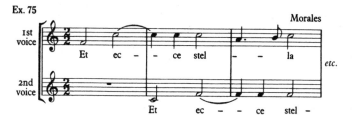

Ex. 75

The first voice's entry in Ex. 75, moving from tonic to dominant, is described as an AUTHENTIC version of the tune, while the second voice's entry, moving from dominant to tonic, is called PLAGAL.

This adjustment was seldom needed in stepwise tunes. The tonic–dominant pull was not so obvious and they could more easily be carried across or TRANSPOSED to a different level without losing their original shape. But tunes with a B♭ in them needed an E♭ in the answering voice, as in Ex. 76 :

Ex. 76

And tunes with a B, when transposed, needed to have the F in the answering voice raised a semitone, or SHARPENED. The sign for a SHARP is ♯. It is written before the note, at the appropriate line or space, as in the answer in Ex. 77 :

Ex. 77

(Today we can sharpen or flatten any note we like, but in sixteenth-century counterpoint the only sharpened notes were F♯, C♯ and G♯, and the only flattened notes were B♭ and E♭ ; other sharps or flats were exceptional.)

Sharps were very often needed at cadences, for composers found that the semitone below the tonic had an irresistible power of drawing the music home.   Because of this power, the major seventh of a scale is often referred to as the LEADING NOTE :

Ex. 78

Josquin

Ad   te   so - lum ———— con - fu - - gi - mus.

(At the beginning of Ex. 78 there is no need to repeat the flat sign for the second and third notes : a flat or sharp in front of a note is still active *during the remainder of the bar it is in*.)

A sharpened or flattened note is sometimes changed, a few notes further on, to the level of the ' natural ' white-note scale : an F sharp, for instance, can be followed in the same bar by an F NATURAL, or a B flat can be followed by a B NATURAL. The sign for a natural is ♮.   It is written before the note, as in Ex. 79 :

Ex. 79

be - ne - di - ctus,

The freedom of choice in sharps, flats, or naturals gradually led music away from the restrictions of the ' white-note ' modes and added to the excitement of sixteenth-century counterpoint.

Renaissance composers were seldom satisfied with writing actual ' note-against-note ' music for long at a stretch ; they found it too uneventful.   In their short phrases of note-against-note they could use only consonant intervals, perfect and imperfect, as in Ex. 80 :

Ex. 80

There is no interval of a fourth in Ex. 80 because in sixteenth-century two-part counterpoint the perfect fourth was considered to be a dissonance. This may seem puzzling, for in itself the *isolated* interval remains a perfect consonance. But music is never static, and when a perfect fourth is heard in relation to the other intervals the upper note very often sounds as if it were wanting to move down a semitone and become a major third. This 'wanting to move elsewhere' makes it sound dissatisfied, so it has to be treated as if it were a dissonance. (Fourths can be used note-against-note in the upper voices of counterpoint in three or more parts, because the interval only sounds dissatisfied when it is formed with the lowest voice.)

Sixteenth-century composers used parallel, oblique, and contrary motion in their counterpoint, but they greatly preferred contrary motion to either of the others, because it had far more opportunities for independence.

In parallel motion they used only imperfect consonances (thirds and sixths) :

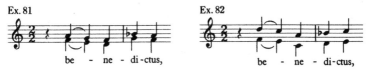

Ex. 81   Ex. 82

be - ne - di -ctus,   be - ne - di -ctus,

Perfect consonances were never used in parallel motion in Renaissance counterpoint, because these intervals, being so strong in themselves, could reinforce a melodic line and make it stand out too prominently for independent part-writing. Composers therefore avoided parallel or CONSECUTIVE octaves

or fifths.   They also avoided parallel fourths with the bass,
but they used them between upper parts :

Dissonances, in the sixteenth century, were never allowed to
drift up and down in parallel motion.   This was because a
dissonance, owing to its uncomfortable tension, always longs
to relax, or RESOLVE to a consonance.   Without its RESOLUTION,
a DISCORD has no meaning in Renaissance counterpoint.

CHAPTER 18

THE SMOOTH RESOLUTION OF DISSONANCE

THE most frequently used dissonance in Renaissance counterpoint is the PASSING-NOTE, which is a dissonant note moving
stepwise up or down from one consonance to another.   The
dissonance is always *between* the beats of the bar : the notes
either side of it, which are *on* the beat, are always consonant.
A passing-note always continues to move in the same direction
in which it started.   (In Ex. 84 and the following examples
the passing-notes are marked ★.)

‡ Exs. 84-90 are taken from the two-voice motets of Lassus.

An AUXILIARY NOTE, like a passing-note, is a dissonant note moving stepwise up or down to a consonance, but instead of continuing to move in the same direction in which it started, the auxiliary note turns back to the note it has just left. (In Ex. 85 and the following examples the auxiliary note is marked †.)

Ex. 85

An ANTICIPATION is a short dissonant note which moves down stepwise from a consonance, anticipating the arrival of the note it is moving towards. (In Ex. 86 the anticipation is marked ⨯.)

Ex. 86

An ACCENTED PASSING-NOTE is a dissonant note moving stepwise downwards. Unlike the ordinary passing-note, the accented passing-note, marked ⊕ in Ex. 87, is dissonant *on* the beat. The short note that follows it is always consonant :

Ex. 87

In sixteenth-century music accented passing-notes are most often used on the WEAK beats, that is, the second or fourth beats of a quadruple bar.

The only sixteenth-century dissonance that occurs on the strong beat is the SUSPENSION.   This is a device that delays the arrival of the note that really belongs to the interval.   It brings the excitement of tension to intervals which might otherwise sound too relaxed in their unperturbed consonance. And it brings the excitement of syncopation to a time-pattern which might otherwise sound too stodgily uneventful.   In Ex. 88, for instance, the counterpoint is satisfactory but somewhat mild :

Ex. 88

This is considerably enlivened if the upper voice is held up so that it arrives a crotchet late, as in Ex. 88A :

Ex. 88a

The tied notes in Ex. 88A are suspensions.   A suspension can never be thought of statically ;   like everything else in music *it has to be heard while moving.*   In Ex. 88B (of which Ex. 88A is a simplified version) the suspensions move forward with greater urgency, for the composer introduces an anticipation before each resolution, and embellishes the final resolution with an anticipation and an auxiliary :

Ex. 88b

The lower voice in Ex. 88B enlivens the rhythm still further by moving stepwise to a new consonance and then leaping off it to the next strong beat of the bar.

CHAPTER 19

LEAPS

LEAPS in sixteenth-century counterpoint are always to and from a consonance, as in Ex. 89 :

Ex. 89

etc.

(The leaps in Ex. 88b may *look* as if they are landing on discords, but this is because of the delayed arrival of the syncopated intervals.)

The only dissonance that is left by leap is the CAMBIATA, or ' changed ' note : it is the second of a group of four short notes making a pattern as in Ex. 90, (the cambiata is marked ' c.') :

Ex. 90

etc.

Quick leaps are rare in the church music of sixteenth-century composers, but they are often found in their secular works. In Ex. 91 the cheerful downward leap of a fourth, repeated at a new level in each bar of the tune, brings a marked emphasis to the words :

Ex. 91

(Sixteenth-century singers would have had no written bar lines in Ex. 91. In writing the tune in modern notation the first voice is not given the conventional grouping of a crotchet tied to a quaver : the unusual grouping shows at a glance that the rhythm itself is unusual.)

The entry of the second and third voices in imitation comes so closely on the heels of the first voice that it almost knocks it off its balance by introducing a conflicting pulse. This VARIED PULSE RHYTHM can only be used in short sentences, as its exuberance is too breathless to be kept up for long.

Many of the quick secular songs of the Renaissance are in simpler, dance-like rhythms, with the voices abandoning their usual imitation and moving together in HOMOPHONIC, or 'same-sounding' time-patterns, as in Ex. 92 :

Ex. 92

In this song the composer is not only concerned with listening horizontally to the interweaving of the different lines of melody : he is also concerned with listening vertically to the combined intervals on the first and third beats of every bar.

These combined intervals are called CHORDS. (It is useful to remember that an interval consists of only two notes and a chord consists of more than two notes.)

Moving from one chord to another is HARMONY.

Part V. Chords

CHAPTER 20

TRIADS

THERE is no fixed boundary between harmony and counter-point. Chords can grow out of tunes, and tunes can grow out of chords. The sprightly 'Fa-la-las' in Ex. 92 move in vertical blocks of chords, but while the song is being sung the singers are chiefly aware of their own horizontal lines of melody.

Singing rounds is one of the easiest ways of learning to listen both vertically and horizontally. If the Elizabethan round for four voices in Ex. 93 is sung in unison, the music consists of nothing but a tune :

Ex. 93 *   16th century

The white hen she cack-les and lays in the pud-dle. Sing
hey! Cock with-out a comb, Cock - a - doo lud - dle.

* If this is too high, sing it an octave lower.

When each of the four voices in Ex. 93 enters one after the other, a bar apart, the listener is chiefly aware of two chords persistently marking the main beats in every bar. (Ex. 93A shows the alternative way of writing out Ex. 93 : it makes it easier to recognise what is happening vertically.)

The two persistent chords are the combined intervals that arrive on the first and on the fourth quavers of the bar, as shown in Ex. 93B :

Since the tonic in Ex. 93 is C, and the dominant is G, the two chords in Ex. 93B can be described as the CHORD OF THE DOMINANT followed by the CHORD OF THE TONIC.

The C-to-C scale was the mode that became increasingly popular at the end of the sixteenth century. Its pattern in tones and semitones is now known by the name of MAJOR SCALE.

The Dorian, Phrygian, Lydian and Mixolydian modes went out of fashion in the seventeenth century, and the only other scale that was used was a modified version of the Aeolian mode, called the MINOR SCALE.

Each degree of a major or minor scale has its own name, which describes its relation to the tonic.

Ex. 94

Major scale of C

| Tonic | Super-tonic | Mediant | Sub-dominant | Dominant | Sub-mediant | Leading-note | Tonic |

(The TONIC SOL-FA names of DOH, RAY, ME, FAH, SOH, LAH, TE are sometimes used as alternatives to the names in Ex. 94.)

Every scale degree has its own chord:

Ex. 94a

C is Tonic

| Tonic | Super-tonic | Mediant | Sub-dominant | Dominant | Sub-mediant | Leading-note |

These three-note chords are called TRIADS. A triad consists of any note of a scale with the third above it and the fifth above it. A triad is described as major or minor according to whether the third above the scale degree is major or minor. In a major scale the triads on the tonic, subdominant, and dominant are MAJOR TRIADS and the triads on the supertonic, mediant, and submediant are MINOR TRIADS. The triad on the leading note is a DIMINISHED TRIAD because the fifth above the leading note is diminished.

The written sign for a triad on any note of a scale is a Roman numeral, corresponding to the scale degree, with a small $\frac{5}{3}$ after it to show that the chord consists of the third and the fifth above the lowest note, or BASS note. Ex. 94A can be written C. $I\frac{5}{3}$ $II\frac{5}{3}$ $III\frac{5}{3}$ $IV\frac{5}{3}$ $V\frac{5}{3}$ $VI\frac{5}{3}$ $VII\frac{5}{3}$.

Closely-packed triads are no use for HARMONIZING a tune: they have to be freed from the tight bundle of notes and allowed to spread themselves into well-spaced chords. (A quick way of proving this is to try to play ' God save the Queen ' using nothing but the bunched-up parallel triads in Ex. 94A.)

Well-spaced chords often extend below the range of the treble clef : their lowest notes are real bass notes. It is therefore necessary to learn to recognize all the bass-clef notes in Ex. 95 :

Ex. 95

C D E F G A B c d e f g a b c' d' e' f' g'

(The line for the F below middle C (*f*) is already clearly defined by its clef sign. Learn *g* and *a* above it. Then learn *e* and *d* below it. Practise these five notes, and when they are familiar go further up and down. *Always hear what you are learning*, just as if you were practising the pronunciation of the written vocabulary of a foreign language.)

SPACED chords are very often four-note chords, with one of the three notes of the triad DOUBLED at the octave or the unison. Ex. 96 shows half-a-dozen possible SPACINGS of the tonic triad of C, with the tonic as the DOUBLED NOTE :

Ex. 96

$$I\frac{5}{3} \quad I\frac{5}{3} \quad I\frac{5}{3} \quad I\frac{5}{3} \quad I\frac{5}{3} \quad I\frac{5}{3}$$

(There are many other possible spacings. The third and the fifth can be in *any* position above the lowest note : the $\frac{5}{3}$ is only a symbol to show that the third and fifth must be there somewhere.)

The TONIC TRIAD is sometimes called the COMMON CHORD. This is a mistranslation of the Latin word ' ordinarius ', which in this case does not mean ' ordinary ' but ' orderly '.

The orderliness of a common chord refers to one of the laws of acoustics. When a note is played on the piano, its string, which has been tightened to produce a certain frequency, vibrates for the whole of its length.   But, at the same time, it vibrates in sections of a half, a third, a quarter and so on.   Each of these sections produces a faint, ghostly note of its own, according to its frequency. These faint notes are called HARMONICS, or OVERTONES, or PARTIALS. If the note that is played is C, two octaves below *c'*, the HARMONIC SERIES of faint notes will be those shown in Ex. 97.   (The harmonics in brackets are slightly out of tune.)

Ex. 97

The higher harmonics are inaudible, which is a blessing, because they would jangle in an unbearable discord.   But the 2nd, 3rd, 4th, 5th and 6th harmonics can be heard, *very* faintly, if the FUNDAMENTAL C is played on the piano with the pedal held down.   These audible harmonics are the notes of the COMMON CHORD OF C.

CHAPTER 21

CADENCES

EXPLORING harmony means listening not only to the tune but also *to the way one bass note follows another* :

Ex. 98

The bass notes in Ex. 98 fit the tune so well that they sound inevitable. Choosing which of the possible triads to use is a matter of skill and experience. For a beginning, it is as well to get used to the sound and feel of two or three chords at a time. The relationship between the tonic chord and the dominant chord is the first to explore, for it is the most important in all harmony, owing to the magnetic pull between the tonic and dominant in a tune, mentioned on page 16.

In Ex. 99 these two chords provide quite a satisfactory harmonization. (The spacing is arranged to suit two hands on a piano) :

Ex. 99

A tune's sense of home-coming at its final cadence can sound even more expressive when heard with the appropriate cadence in the harmony. The HARMONIC CADENCE at the last two bars of Ex. 99, where the music moves from the dominant chord to the chord of the tonic, is described as a PERFECT CADENCE.

The cadence at the end of the first and second sections of Ex. 99, where there is a ' half-close ' that moves from tonic to dominant, is described as an IMPERFECT CADENCE.

When learning to harmonize with three chords instead of two, the easiest new chord to choose is the chord of the subdominant, as this is the next in importance. In Ex. 100 it brings a welcome change from Ex. 99's perpetual to-and-fro of tonic and dominant :

Ex. 100

The harmony in bars 10 and 12 of Ex. 100, where the subdominant chord moves to the tonic chord, is described as a PLAGAL CADENCE.

There is a fourth cadence in harmony, in addition to the perfect, imperfect, and plagal cadences. It is called the INTERRUPTED cadence. It is used as a comma in the music, never as a full stop. It begins like a perfect cadence with the chord of the dominant, but then it changes its mind and moves to an unexpected chord, very often the chord of the submediant, as in Ex. 101 :

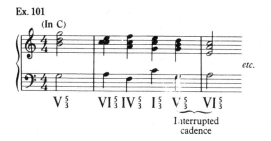

Interrupted
cadence

CHAPTER 22

INVERSIONS

THE C major tune in Ex. 102 is harmonized with six of the seven notes of the scale as bass notes :

The missing scale degree is the leading note : it is often avoided as a bass note because of the discomfort of its diminished fifth. This does not mean, however, that the triad belonging to the seventh note of the scale can never be used. It is frequently used with the actual leading note in a different position.

Triads, like intervals, can be INVERTED. In Ex. 94A, on page 70, where the note which the chord belongs to is in the bass, the triads are in ROOT POSITION. If each triad in Ex. 94A is turned upside-down by taking the lowest note and moving it up an octave, the result is a row of FIRST INVERSIONS :

Ex. 94b

C I $^6_3$ II $^6_3$ III $^6_3$ IV $^6_3$ V $^6_3$ VI $^6_3$ VII $^6_3$

The Roman numerals in Ex. 94B represent the *root* of the chord, which has now been banished from the bass : the figure $^6_3$ represents the intervals of the third and the sixth above the *lowest note* of the chord.

Heard one after another, these first inversions in Ex. 94B sound much more satisfactory for harmonizing than the bunched-up root positions in Ex. 94A. The parallel fourths in the upper parts are not so obviously reinforcing the notes of the scale as the consecutive fifths. In harmony, as in counterpoint, parts need to sound independent. For this reason, consecutive fourths are only used in the upper parts, and consecutive octaves and fifths are not used at all:

Ex. 103

(In C)

etc.

VI $^6_3$ V $^6_3$ IV $^6_3$ III $^6_3$ II $^6_3$ I $^6_3$ VII $^6_3$ I $^5_3$

When spacing first inversions as four-note chords, the doubled notes have to be chosen very carefully to avoid using 'forbidden consecutives', especially if there are several chords one after another in parallel motion. In Ex. 94B, if either the lowest note or the third or the sixth were to be doubled in every chord, the result would be a row of consecutive octaves and fifths. Therefore composers double the notes of first inversions alternately. (See Ex. 103.)

The VII $\frac{6}{3}$ in Ex. 103 is a dissonant chord : it can only be used when passing smoothly by step from one consonance to another. (The consecutive fifths between the two upper voices are not 'forbidden', since only one of the fifths is perfect : they can therefore be used in SIMILAR MOTION.)

Many of the customs or 'rules' of counterpoint apply equally to harmony. For instance, the interval of a fourth above the bass has to be treated as a dissonance. A chord can be written with the fourth and the sixth above the lowest note :

But in harmony a $\frac{6}{4}$ CHORD cannot be used on its own, because the fourth from the bass makes it sound unsatisfied, and it will have to move somewhere else in order to resolve. When it moves where it wants to go, it makes sense as harmony, as in Ex. 104:

Ex. 104
(In C)   Dowland

$I\frac{5}{3}$ $I\frac{5}{3}$ $IV\frac{5}{3}$ $V\frac{6}{4}-\frac{5}{3}$ $I\frac{5}{3}$

The $\frac{6}{4}$ chord is often referred to as a SECOND INVERSION. This can be misleading, because in the language of 'strict' harmony the sound is incomplete and it cannot represent a triad until it has been completed. In Ex. 104 the root of the chord is not the tonic but the dominant : the smooth descending crotchets are *accented passing-notes*, inherited from counterpoint. This $\frac{6}{4}-\frac{5}{3}$ progression is so often used in cadences that it is referred to as a CADENTIAL $\frac{6}{4}$.

In the last bar of Ex. 104, and also at the end of Ex. 103, the I_3^5 chord is without its interval of a fifth.   This often happens in harmony, particularly at a final cadence where the tune comes to rest on the tonic.   In the sixteenth and seventeenth centuries either the third or the fifth could be left out of a $_3^5$ chord when necessary, but the third is never left out in the eighteenth century, which is the period from which beginners learn most about harmony.

Part VI. Key Relationships

CHAPTER 23

TRANSPOSITION

EIGHTEENTH-CENTURY composers of four-part harmony usually wrote their voice parts for SOPRANO, ALTO, TENOR and BASS, using a stave for each voice, that is, in OPEN SCORE, with the C clef for the alto and the tenor. (We now use the treble clef for the alto, and the treble clef *an octave higher than it sounds* for the tenor.)

Today we frequently use only two staves for the four voices, writing in SHORT SCORE with the alto in the treble clef and the tenor in the bass clef. This saves space, but it means using a good many leger lines when the notes are particularly high or low.

The approximate compass for a SOPRANO (the top voice, above the others) is

The ALTO's compass is

(This is the highest part that a man can sing. A male alto is sometimes called a COUNTER-TENOR. The correct name for a female alto is a CONTRALTO.)

The compass of a TENOR in four-part harmony is
(The name ' tenor ' is inherited from medieval counterpoint, when the voice ' held ' the notes of the tune.)

The compass of a BASS is

(A high bass who can sing above the *d'* but cannot reach down to the *F* is called a BARITONE.)

In many pieces of music the compass would be either too high or too low if C had to be the tonic.   Ex. 101, for instance, is too high for comfort, particularly for the tenors.   Fortunately there is an easy way of bringing it down to a more comfortable pitch, for the pattern of the C-to-C scale can be moved up or down to any level.   The only thing that needs adjusting is the position of the semitones, which must always be between the mediant and the subdominant, and between the leading note and the tonic.   This can be done by adding sharps or flats.

The process of moving up or down is called TRANSPOSITION. Polyphonic writers of the sixteenth century had already discovered that they could make their Mixolydian G-to-G scale the same shape as the C scale by sharpening its seventh note, F.   And they could make their Lydian F-to-F scale the same shape as C-to-C by flattening its fourth note, B.   There was no need to write the ♯ in front of every F or the ♭ in front of every B ; they just wrote an F sharp or a B flat at the beginning of the piece of music.   This labour-saving device is called a KEY SIGNATURE : it is written immediately after the clef at the beginning of each new line of music.   (The time signature follows the key signature : it is only written once, in the opening line.)

🎼♯ is the key signature of G MAJOR : it shows that every F throughout the piece of music, at whatever octave it occurs, is to be sharpened.

🎼♭ is the key signature of F MAJOR : it shows that every B, at any octave, is to be flattened.

Music that is founded on the scale of G major is in the KEY of G.

Music founded on the scale of F major is in the key of F.

The triads in Ex. 94A can be transposed into G or into F and used as the basis of harmonizing tunes in G or F.   Cadences in G and F soon become familiar if Exs. 99, 100 and 102 are transposed down a fourth for G and down a fifth for F. (Think of the written C in these examples as a symbol for I, the written G as a symbol for V and the written F as a symbol for IV. Begin by playing the bass only, in the transposed key. Hear in your mind's ear the chords that go with the bass, and try and find the notes for them, remembering the F♯ for the key of G and the B♭ for the key of F. It will then be possible to follow the harmony in Exs. 105 and 106 in the keys in which they are written.)

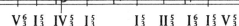

Chapter 24

RELATIVE MINORS

Tunes are not always in a major key. A great many are
founded on the modified version of the Aeolian mode called
the minor scale. This has two forms, the Melodic and the
Harmonic.

The Melodic Minor Scale begins like the Aeolian mode,
but sharpens the sixth and seventh notes when going up.
(See the first half of Ex. 107.) Coming down, the scale is
exactly the same as the Aeolian mode :

Ex. 107

A minor, melodic

The Harmonic Minor Scale is the same as the Aeolian
mode except for the seventh note, which is sharpened going
up and coming down :

Ex. 107a

A minor, harmonic

The unusually large step between the sixth and seventh notes
in the harmonic minor scale is an Augmented Second,
measuring a tone and a half.

The triads on the scale degrees of A minor, harmonic and
melodic, are shown in Ex. 107b—d :

Ex. 107b

Harmonic minor triads

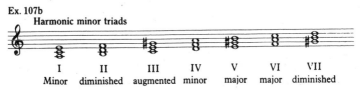

I	II	III	IV	V	VI	VII
Minor	diminished	augmented	minor	major	major	diminished

Ex. 107c

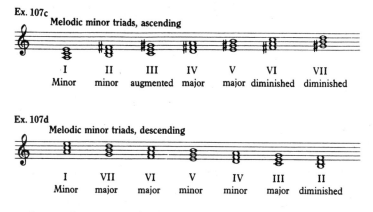

Melodic minor triads, ascending

	I	II	III	IV	V	VI	VII
	Minor	minor	augmented	major	major	diminished	diminished

Ex. 107d

Melodic minor triads, descending

	I	VII	VI	V	IV	III	II
	Minor	major	major	minor	minor	major	diminished

The triad on III in the harmonic minor and the ascending melodic minor scale is called an AUGMENTED TRIAD because the interval between the mediant and the leading note is an AUGMENTED FIFTH. Augmented triads, like diminished triads, are dissonances. They are used in their $\frac{6}{3}$ position more often than in their root position. They always pass smoothly in stepwise movement from one consonance to another. ('Always' refers to eighteenth-century harmony.)

Minor tunes can be harmonized with any of the triads in Ex. 107B—D. The final perfect cadence always has the sharpened leading note, as in Ex. 108 :

Ex. 108

Key of A minor   German, 16th century

(In Ex. 108 and the examples in the following chapters the figure $\frac{5}{3}$ is not given, because the root position is always taken for granted in FIGURED HARMONY whenever the chord is without a figure. Roman numerals are only used for extra guidance in the early stages of learning harmony.)

The sharps written under the chords in Ex. 108 show that the third in the $\frac{5}{3}$ chord is to be sharpened.

The major third in the tonic chord at the end of the minor tune in Ex. 108 is characteristic of nearly all the music written between 1500 and 1750.   Medieval counterpoint ended on the combined intervals of the fifth and the octave—what we now call the ' bare ' fifth, because to our ears it sounds naked.   In the early sixteenth century, when composers began using the third in their cadences, they preferred to end their modal music with a major third rather than the minor third belonging to the mode.   (It is possible that when listening to the sound of a bare-fifth cadence dying away in one of their vast, resonant cathedrals, they may have heard the faint suggestion of the major third in the harmonic series, joining in like a ghostly extra voice.   What is certain is that they liked the sound of this beautiful cadence, which, for some unknown reason, is often called by the inappropriate name of ' tierce de Picardie '.)

Every minor key is related to a major key.   C major and A minor share the same key signature, therefore A minor is described as the RELATIVE MINOR of C major.

Every major key has its relative minor which shares the same key signature.

The tonic of the minor scale is the submediant of its relative major.

The relative minor of G major is E minor ; it has F♯ in the key signature, and its sixth and seventh notes are sharpened to C♯ and D♯ when necessary.

The relative minor of F major is D minor ; it has B♭ in the key signature, and its sixth and seventh notes are sharpened to B♮ and C♯ when necessary. (The words ' sharpened ' and ' flattened ' mean ' raised a semitone ', and ' lowered a semitone ', so there is nothing incongruous in finding a note sharpened to a natural.)

The additional sharps to the sixth and seventh notes of these scales are called ACCIDENTALS, as they are only used on certain occasions.   An accidental is any sharp, flat, or natural that is not given in the key signature.   An accidental in front of a note applies as often as the note is repeated *at that particular octave during the remainder of the bar it is in*. In the bar that comes after accidental sharps or flats it is usual to find ' warning' naturals to contradict the accidentals in the previous bar. These 'warning' signs are only used when there is likely to be any doubt in the mind of the singer or player : they are sometimes written with brackets round them, as in the harmonic minor scale in Ex. 107A.

CHAPTER 25

THE CIRCLE OF FIFTHS

ANY note can be chosen as the tonic or KEY-NOTE of a scale. The key signatures of the different major keys are easy to learn if they are taken in the right order.

The order of the SHARP KEYS goes up in fifths. The dominant of one key becomes the tonic of the next key. The newly acquired sharp is always the seventh note of the scale.
C has no sharps
    (The dominant of C is G) ;
G has 1 sharp, F♯
    (The dominant of G is D) ;
D has 2 sharps, F♯, C♯
    (The dominant of D is A) ;
A has 3 sharps, F♯, C♯, G♯
    (The dominant of A is E) ;
E has 4 sharps, F♯, C♯, G♯, D♯
    (The dominant of E is B) ;
B has 5 sharps, F♯, C♯, G♯, D♯, A♯
    (The dominant of B is F♯) ;
F♯ has 6 sharps, F♯, C♯, G♯, D♯, A♯, E♯
    (The dominant of F♯ is C♯) ;
C♯ has 7 sharps, F♯, C♯, G♯, D♯, A♯, E♯, B♯).

The order of the FLAT KEYS goes *down* in fifths. The tonic of one key becomes the dominant of the next. The newly acquired flat is always the fourth note of the scale.

C has no flats

(C is the dominant of F) ;

F has 1 flat, B♭

(F is the dominant of B♭) ;

B♭ has 2 flats, B♭, E♭

(B♭ is the dominant of E♭) ;

E♭ has 3 flats, B♭, E♭, A♭

(E♭ is the dominant of A♭) ;

A♭ has 4 flats, B♭, E♭, A♭, D♭

(A♭ is the dominant of D♭).

D♭ has 5 flats, B♭, E♭, A♭, D♭, G♭.

With the help of key signatures, the pattern of the scale of C in Ex. 94 can be transposed to all the sharp and flat keys. When this is tried out on the piano, the key note of C♯ is at exactly the same level of pitch as the key note of D♭. This is because the twelve semitones dividing the octave on the piano —seven white notes and five black notes—all have alternative names, according to whether they are being used in a sharp key or a flat key. For instance, the black note a semitone below A is G♯ in the scale of A and A♭ in the key of E♭. And the white note F becomes E♯ in the key of F♯. (White-note sharps are no different from black-note sharps. The only reason they look like that is because the pattern of black and white on the piano has been designed to suit the comfort of the pianist's fingers and thumbs.)

Altering the letter-name of a note without altering its level of pitch, as with G♯ to A♭, is referred to as an ENHARMONIC CHANGE.

The CIRCLE OF FIFTHS on page 87 shows all the key signatures with the correct level of octave on the stave for writing each sharp or flat. It also shows each relative minor sharing the same key-signature with its relative major.

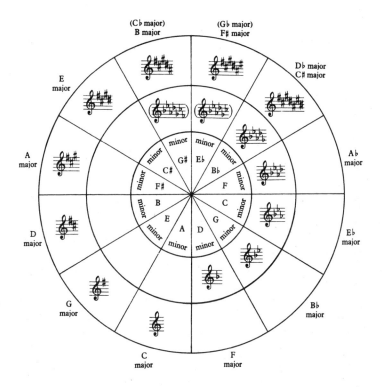

The keys of G♭ major and C♭ major are shown in brackets because they are so seldom used. E♭ minor is more often used than D♯ minor, because minor keys with a lot of sharps become involved in DOUBLE SHARPS. For example, the sharpened leading note of G♯ minor is a semitone higher than F♯ : it is called ' F double sharp ' and is written : F✗.

DOUBLE FLATS are written ♭♭.

Key signatures are an important part of the grammar of music, and, like the grammar of any other language, they need to be learnt by their sound and their feel, not only by their written appearance.   If the scales in Exs. 94, 107 and 107A, and the cadences in Exs. 99, 100, 101 and 104, and the chords in Exs. 102, 103, 105 and 106 are explored in each of the sharp and flat keys, it becomes easier to read music that is written in any key.   It also becomes possible to understand what happens when a piece of music moves away from its own key and enters another key.

CHAPTER 26

MODULATION

MOVING from one key to another is called MODULATION, (from the Latin verb ' to adjust '.)

PASSING MODULATIONS are often found in hymn tunes: the music sounds for the moment as if it were going right into another key, but immediately changes its mind and comes back again.

Passing, or ' transitory ' modulations are mostly to RELATED KEYS, that is, to keys that are nearest to each other in the circle of fifths on page 87.

Ex. 109 shows a transitory modulation to the dominant :

Ex. 109   Key of G   German Chorale

In the third bar of Ex. 109 the cadential $^6_4$ opens the door to the new key by introducing D's leading note in a perfect cadence. But the ear can recognize that the tune does not mean to get right inside the key and stay there, for the move sounds too casual to be anything more than a momentary inclination. When this minim chord of D is heard in relation to the whole sentence *it still feels like a dominant*. After the comma, the tune returns to the tonic chord of G without any sense of frustration. And in the following bar the sub-dominant chord of C banishes the temporary C♯ that is no longer wanted.

The hymn in Ex. 110 shows a transitory modulation to the subdominant :

Ex. 110

Key of F

German Chorale

In the second bar of Ex. 110 the chord of E♭ gets rid of the leading note of the key of F. This robs the following F chord of its tonic power and turns it into a temporary dominant of B♭. In the very next bar, however, the chord of C restores the E♮, leaving the ear in no doubt at all about the tune's allegiance to the key of F.

It is no effort at all for a major tune to arrive at the chord of its relative minor, with or without the help of an interrupted cadence. (See Ex. 101 p. 75). But this casual visiting is not modulating. *A modulation to any key has to introduce the unmistakable dominant chord of the new key.*

Ex. 111 shows a transitory modulation to the relative minor :

In Ex. 111 the dominant chord of the new key is the $\frac{6}{3}$ at the end of the first bar : its power lasts until the G♯ is banished by the cadential $\frac{6}{4}$ that brings the harmony back to C.

The power of a dominant chord becomes even more compelling if it is turned into a DOMINANT SEVENTH.

The DOMINANT SEVENTH CHORD began life as a passing-note in Renaissance counterpoint :

This smooth, expressive way of linking the notes of the perfect cadence became so familiar that its four notes—DOMINANT, LEADING NOTE, SUPERTONIC and SUBDOMINANT—were accepted as a chord.

It was called ' the chord of the dominant seventh ' because of the interval of a seventh from the dominant up to the subdominant.

The root position of a dominant seventh chord is written in figures as $\frac{7}{5}$. Its first inversion is $\frac{6}{5}$, second inversion $\frac{6}{4}$ and
third inversion $\frac{6}{4}$.

The hymn in Ex. 113 shows the dominant seventh chord of C in its root position, first inversion, second inversion and third inversion :

Ex. 113
Key of C   German Chorale

The dominant seventh chord, being dissonant, has to resolve smoothly by step.   (See the resolutions in Ex. 113.)

The dissonance of a dominant seventh chord is partly caused by the minor seventh between the dominant and the subdominant, but it is much more the result of the tritone between the leading note and the subdominant.

In a $\frac{6}{5}$ the tritone with the bass is a diminished fifth, which longs to resolve *inwards* by step.

In a $\frac{6}{4}$ the tritone with the bass is an augmented fourth, which longs to resolve *outwards* by step.

In the $\frac{7}{5}$ and the $\frac{6}{4}$ the tritone is in the upper parts, so the dissonance is not so piercing.   But whatever the spacing may be, the resolutions sound smoother when the diminished fifth moves inwards and the augmented fourth outwards.

Dominant seventh chords are shared by a major key and its
TONIC MINOR, that is, by the minor key that has the same
letter-name, (C major, C minor, etc.) :

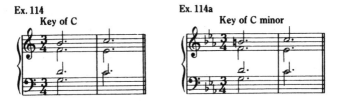

Finding the dominant seventh chord and its resolutions in all
the keys involves trying it with various spacings as a perfect
cadence in each major key and each tonic minor.   This takes
time, but the labour is worth it in the end, even though the
solid slabs of chords have no meaning outside a musical sentence.
The real meaning of a dominant seventh chord, like everything
else in music, can only be recognized when heard in its context, as in Ex. 115, where it provides a dramatic opening for
one of Bach's most expressive hymns :

Part VII. Harmonization

CHAPTER 27

DISSONANCES IN EIGHTEENTH-CENTURY HARMONY

HYMNS, or CHORALES, are often used for studying eighteenth-century harmony. This is not only because they are short enough to prevent the learner getting discouraged. It is also because they have a clearly defined cadence at the end of each line. A Bach chorale can be studied in sections, for each short section is an eventful journey towards its cadence. The four voices move together at each word, which makes the chords easier to recognize than some of the more scattered harmonies in instrumental music.

Harmony uses the same devices as counterpoint for introducing the tension of discord. Ex. 116 shows how unaccented passing-notes can link the chords of a simple harmonic structure :

Ex. 116

The chords in Ex. 116 can be played without their quaver passing-notes, and the music will still make sense. In harmony, as in counterpoint, there has to be a firm and satisfying foundation to support any embellishments. Passing-notes are no help if the CHORDAL STRUCTURE is weak.

Suspensions are used in harmony just as much as in counterpoint. They are no longer restricted to the main beats of the bar :

Auxiliary notes (marked †) and anticipations (✴) are also borrowed from counterpoint, as in Ex. 118, where they enrich the cadential $^6_4$:

In harmony, as in counterpoint, all dissonances have to resolve by step, therefore leaping on or off a discord is ' forbidden '. There are two exceptions : first, the cambiata, which need not keep to exactly the same pattern as in counterpoint :

The other exception is the quaver leap from a dissonance shown in Ex. 120. This is called an ÉCHAPPÉE. The first quaver 'escapes' from its chord and moves to a note belonging to the following chord :

(The difference between the échappée and the cambiata is that the échappée moves away from the direction in which the voice means to go, while the cambiata moves in the same direction, but goes too far and has to come back again.)

Accented passing-notes are used far more often in harmony than in counterpoint :

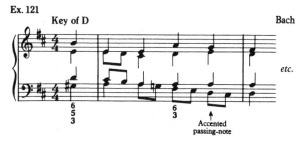

The accented passing-note in Ex. 121 is leaning on a first inversion of the dominant seventh, and the delayed arrival of the C♯ makes the chord sound even more expressive than usual.

The examples in this chapter can only sound expressive when they are phrased rhythmically. Harmony cannot exist without rhythm.   A cadential $^6_4$ only makes sense when it is phrased with a stress on the $^6_4$ and a relaxation on the $^5_3$, as in Ex. 122, where the rhythm of the harmony in the last line of the chorale disregards the bar-lines and follows the rhythm of the words :

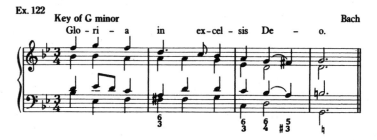

Ex. 122

Key of G minor   Bach

Glo - ri - a   in   ex-cel - sis   De —   o.

CHAPTER 28

CHROMATIC HARMONY

In the ' Gloria in excelsis ' at the end of the last chapter, the bass moves in semitones from F♮ to F♯ to G. Music that moves up or down in semitones is described as CHROMATIC (from the Greek word which means not only ' colour ' but also ' complexion ' and ' modification ').

The semitone from F♮ to F♯ is called a CHROMATIC SEMITONE because the notes never occur one after another in a major or minor scale. (The notes of a chromatic semitone have the same letter-names.)

The semitone from F♯ to G is a DIATONIC SEMITONE because it occurs in diatonic major or minor scales. (The notes of a diatonic semitone always have different letter-names.)

The CHROMATIC SCALE is a twelve-note scale consisting entirely of semitones. It passes through all the twelve notes that are used in Western music. The sound can be heard on the piano by playing up or down through every black and white note between one octave and the next :

Ex. 123

(When a chromatic scale is written with the tonic and the dominant as the two notes whose letter-names occur only once, as in Ex. 123, it is called a ' harmonic chromatic scale '. This name is useful in examinations, but nowhere else. In real music the composer uses sharps or flats according to the shape of the phrase and its harmonic structure.)

The notes of the chromatic scale were not used as the raw material for making tunes until the early twentieth century. Before that they were used for dipping into, in order to colour the diatonic outlines of a journey towards a cadence, as in Ex. 124 :

Ex. 124

The chord at the end of the second bar of Ex. 124 is called the DIMINISHED SEVENTH CHORD because of the interval from G♯ up to F♮, which is a semitone smaller than a minor seventh. (The melodic interval of the diminished seventh came into being as soon as tunes were founded on the harmonic minor scale. It is the inversion of the augmented second between the sixth and seventh notes of the scale.)

The diminished seventh chord can be one of the most expressive sounds in music, yet the chord *by itself* is utterly non-committal. This is because of its shape. It consists of two interlocked tritones. When the chord is heard in isolation the result is a deadlock. Both tritones have latent possibilities for making expressive discords that long to resolve. But neither tritone is able to decide where it wants to go until some other note, from outside the chord, draws it into relation with a tonic. In Ex. 124 the ' other note ' is the anticipating quaver E. This note transforms the diminished seventh into the dominant seventh ($\frac{6}{3}$) of A, which longs to resolve.

If the chord G♯–B–D–F is taken out of its context in Ex. 124, there are many other ways in which it can be compelled to move. For instance, if the G♯ is lowered to G♮ the chord becomes an entirely different dominant seventh and cries out to resolve to C. Or if the G♯ is enharmonically changed to A♭, and the B♮ is lowered to B♭, the chord is transformed to the dominant seventh ($\frac{6}{2}$) of E♭. It is possible, with the help of the diminished seventh chord, to modulate to any key in the circle of fifths, however distantly related, as, for example, in the swift journey from C major to A♭ major in Ex. 125 :

Ex. 125

etc.

Other chromatic chords used in modulations include the
AUGMENTED SIXTH CHORD, which with C as tonic is either
D♭-F-B♮ (called ' Italian ' in text-books) ; or D♭-F-G-B♮
(' French ') ; or D♭-F-A♭-B♮ (' German ').

Learning to modulate is a help in exploring music but it
cannot teach one how to harmonize. Nor is it any use keeping
to the rules of harmony and avoiding forbidden consecutives
without having a feeling for the structure of the music.
Harmony is not just a piecemeal journey towards a cadence :
it is also an accumulative journey from one cadence to the
next. The sense of wholeness in a complete piece of music is
what is meant by the word FORM.

Part VIII. Form and Texture in Music
of the 16th and 17th Centuries

CHAPTER 29

MUSICAL SHAPES

FORM in music cannot be studied in the same way as form in architecture, because music refuses to keep still. The sounds are only there while the performers are singing or playing ; and when the last note dies away the music has gone. Yet something remains, even though many of the details may be forgotten.

A composer has to find the right notes in the right order if he is to prevent his music floating off into oblivion. Formlessness is the result of too much material and not enough order, therefore one of the most important things in music is *economy*.

The order of the notes in an economical tune can create a satisfying *shape* that stands out in the listener's mind, even at a first hearing.

Many of the folk-songs in Chapters 6 to 10 owe their memorable shape to the use of REPETITION. For instance, Ex. 55 on p. 35 is built on a two-bar phrase which is slightly varied in bars 3—4. Ex. 34 has its repetition in the middle section of the tune, with a contrasting phrase at the beginning and end. Ex. 30 has three four-bar phrases, each of which is different, but the last two bars of the tune are an exact repetition of the first two bars, and this links the end with the beginning in a particularly satisfying way.

This kind of ANALYSIS of the shape of a tune leads to a certain amount of text-book labelling : tunes are described as 'A¹ A²B' or 'ABBC,' without any reference to their rhythm or to the rise and fall of their phrases. A tune cannot be clamped down in a mould as if it were a blancmange. Every piece of music has an individual life of its own, and the only way to study its shape is to get right inside the sound of it, as a student of architecture gets right inside a building.

Composers, like architects, plan the shape of their work according to the purpose for which it has been ordered. Bach harmonized hymn tunes because he earned his living as an organist and had to provide something for the congregation to sing on Sundays.

Every composer thinks of the practical conditions of performance before he begins writing. This means that every piece of music has not only its own shape but also its own TEXTURE.

The word texture is borrowed by musicians because they have so few words for describing their intangible art. They refer to the ' dark colour ' of a piece of music, although there is nothing to be seen with the eyes, and they speak of a ' light texture ' although there is nothing to be felt between the fingers.

' Texture ' can describe the interweaving of horizontal lines in counterpoint or the spacing of vertical chords in harmony. TIMBRE can describe the QUALITY OF TONE of different instruments or voices. ' Colour ' can describe the musical expression in the playing or singing.

CHAPTER 30

16TH-CENTURY FORMS AND TEXTURES

THE texture of sixteenth-century music was very different from the sounds we hear today in orchestral concerts or chamber music recitals. There were no public concerts. The polyphonic masterpieces—the Latin masses and motets, or the English services and anthems—were not meant to be listened to as performances : they were an essential part of the church services, and they were described as A CAPPELLA, ' for the choir of a chapel '. (The term *a cappella* now means ' music for unaccompanied voices ', but in the sixteenth century the texture could include the organ or other instruments.)

Secular polyphonic music was meant for informal singing in the home. MADRIGALS (in the ' mother ' tongue) were sung by friends sitting round a table after a meal ; the mood of the music could vary from ELEGIES and LAMENTS to light-hearted CANZONETS (' little songs ') or dance-like BALLETTS. (The ' fa-la-la ' in Ex. 92, p. 67 is from a Ballett.) Secular rounds, called CATCHES, were also sung informally.

Solo songs were AIRS sung to the LUTE, a quiet, expressive instrument with a varying number of open strings, on which the singer could pluck the fingered ' stopped ' notes of his own sensitive ACCOMPANIMENT.

Sixteenth-century keyboard instruments were used for solos rather than for accompaniments. The CLAVICHORD is .too quiet to be combined with voices, for its strings are gently touched by delicate brass tangents. The HARPSICHORD is more robust : its strings are plucked with a quill and its texture and dynamics can range from a thin whisper to a brilliant full-bodied resonance.   (A small harpsichord, with only one keyboard or Manual, is called a Spinet. Smaller still are the Virginals.)

Most sixteenth-century instrumental music was played by small groups in Consort. A Whole Consort consisted of instruments of the same sort, such as the family of stringed instruments called Viols. They had six strings, tuned, like the lute, in perfect fourths, with a major third in the middle. A set (or 'chest') of viols consisted of treble viols, tenor viols and bass viols.   Even the smallest viols were held downwards, resting against the knees, which is why they were called *da gamba*, ' of the leg ', to distinguish them from the newly invented violins, which were *da braccio*, ' of the arm '.   (The name *viola da gamba* is now used only for the bass viol, which is the equivalent of our cello.)

Consort music was also played on Recorders, which are end-blown flutes with a gentler tone than the modern flute. The usual family of recorders consists of Descant (compass c''—d''''), Treble (f'—g'''), Tenor (c'—c'''), and Bass (f—f'').

The sixteenth-century equivalent of our oboes, called Shawms, were too raucous for consort-music in the home ; they could only be played out of doors or in a large building. Brass instruments also belonged to the open air.   Trumpets had to keep to the ' open ' notes of the harmonic series (see p. 72), which meant that their tunes were high and piercing. Trombones, with their ' slides ', could play all the notes of the scale.   (They were still called by the medieval name Sackbut, meaning ' pull-push '.)

A Broken Consort included instruments from different families.   Composers did not always mention what instrument they had in mind.   Often they just wrote First Voice, Second Voice and so on, leaving it to the players to decide what instruments to use.   Sometimes they combined singing with playing : many madrigals were written ' for voices or viols '.   This meant that the form of the music was usually polyphonic.   Ex. 126 shows the beginning of an instrumental Canzon Da Sonar (' song for sounding ') which has the

appearance of a wordless madrigal, though the timbre of the
brass would have sounded utterly different from vocal music :

Ex. 126   G. Gabrieli

Consorts of viols often chose to play a RICERCAR—the
name means ' to search out ' or ' seek again '—a piece with
polyphonic entries in close imitation. A Ricercar could be
founded on a tune such as ' Bonny Sweet Robin ' in Ex. 127 :

Ex. 127   Traditional

This tune has to be searched for in Ex. 127A :

Ex. 127a   Thomas Simpson

The FANTASIA, or FANCY, was freer than the Ricercar, for there was no need for it to have so many entries of the same tune. Fantasias, however, were still closely packed with contrapuntal devices such as imitation in canon. This kind of imitation is described as FUGAL, from the Latin for ' chasing after ' or ' putting to flight '. The short fragment in Ex. 128 shows each instrument chasing the next :

Ex. 128

CHAPTER 31

16th AND 17th-CENTURY DANCE FORMS

THE most popular instrumental pieces in the sixteenth and seventeenth centuries were the DANCE FORMS that were played for the listeners to dance to. The steps and figures of a dance have just as much influence on a tune as the words of a song, and the patterns of these early dances can often be traced in the rise and fall of the musical phrases.

The dignified PAVANE, in slow duple time, was usually followed by the GALLIARD, a gayer dance in fairly quick triple time. The tune of the Galliard was often a variant of the Pavane's tune, as in Exs. 129 and 129A :

Ex. 129
Pavane
Slow
French, 16th century
etc.

Ex. 129a
Galliard
Fairly quick
etc.

The ALMAN was a moderately slow dance in duple time :

Ex. 130
Alman
Fairly slow
Bull
etc.

The CORANTO had quick running figures in both the dance and the music :

Ex. 131

The JIG (or GIGGE) had an energetic skipping rhythm in $\frac{6}{8}$ or $\frac{12}{8}$:

Ex. 132

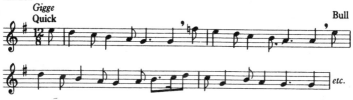

The seventeenth-century HORNPIPE (not to be confused with the later ' Sailor's Hornpipe ') was a dance in triple time with a fair amount of syncopation :

Ex. 133

In the graceful SARABANDE the dancers' second step was often longer than the first :

Ex. 134

The BORRY, in quick duple time, had light runs beginning on an up-beat :

Ex. 135

The MINUET is the best known of all the seventeenth-century dances.   Having begun as a French folk dance, it was introduced at the court of Louis XIV and by the end of the century was being danced all over Europe.   The Minuet in Ex. 136 is called a RONDEAU, because the tune comes round again and again to its first sentence, which is repeated as a REFRAIN :

Ex. 136

CHAPTER 32

SEVENTEENTH-CENTURY VARIATIONS

WHEN seventeenth-century composers wanted to extend the form of their instrumental pieces they often used a dance tune as the foundation of their music. The extended CHACONNE and its near relation the PASSACAGLIA are reminiscent of the poised grace of a Sarabande : the tune in Ex. 137 has the characteristic dotted crotchet on the second beat of the bar :

Ex. 137

The bass part to Ex. 137, called a GROUND, or BASSO OSTINATO, is repeated over and over again throughout the whole piece. (See Ex. 137A).

Ex. 137a

(repeated 15 times)

Seventeenth-century instrumentalists often played DIVI-SIONS ON A GROUND by ' Breaking up ' or ' Dividing ' the long notes of the bass into shorter notes. Ex. 138 shows four of the many possible ways in which they might have broken up the notes D and C :

Ex. 138

Ground

From Christopher Simpson
(The Division Viol.)

This kind of embellishment is called FIGURATION.   The short groups of notes are referred to as FIGURES.   (The word is used in the sense of ' to adorn with '.)

Figuration helped composers to vary the texture of their instrumental works, particularly when they were writing VARIATIONS ON A THEME.   (A tune is known as a THEME when it is extended and developed during a piece of music.)

Exs. 139 to 139c show how Sweelinck and his pupil Scheidt drew out variations from the tune of a well-known Pavane, harmonized by Sweelinck in Ex. 139 :

Ex. 139

Theme: Pavana Hispanica

In Ex. 139A Scheidt invents divisions on the theme :

Ex. 139a

(The rapid figures in Ex. 139A can be thought of as passing notes, auxiliaries and cambiatas which embroider the theme without interfering with the harmony.)

In Ex. 139B Scheidt varies the texture by using the theme contrapuntally in imitation :

Ex. 139b

And in Ex. 139C Sweelinck varies the rhythm of the counterpoint by turning the Pavane into a Galliard :

Ex. 139c

These variations were written for a keyboard instrument and could have been played equally well on an organ or a harpsichord.

Figuration is a characteristic of seventeenth-century keyboard music, particularly in the pieces called TOCCATAS, in which rapid scales alternate with full, resonant chords. The chords were seldom played as solid blocks. They were turned into BROKEN CHORDS, with each of the notes played rhythmically, one after another. Or they were spread out into a cascade of notes called an ARPEGGIO. (A broken chord keeps within the octave : an arpeggio goes beyond it.)

The word toccata (' touch-piece ') referred to the player's fingers touching the keys. It was used in contrast to SONATA ('sound-piece'), which could refer to the sound of viols or violins.

CHAPTER 33

THE TRIO SONATA

THE seventeenth-century sonata, which is very different from the sonatas of Haydn and Mozart, or of Beethoven and Brahms, is sometimes called the BAROQUE SONATA to distinguish it from later sonatas.

There were two different kinds of sonata at the end of the seventeenth century. One was the SONATA DA CAMERA, or chamber sonata, which consisted of several dances, such as Allemande, Courante, Sarabande and Gigue, strung together to make a continuous piece of music. The other was the SONATA DA CHIESA, or church sonata, which had four sections called MOVEMENTS. The first movement was slow and majestic ; the second was quick and lively ; the third was slow and graceful and the fourth was very quick.

These four movements were called by the Italian words that described the character of their different speeds : *Adagio*, slow and leisurely ; *Grave*, slow and solemn ; *Largo*, slow and stately ; *Allegro*, quick and cheerful ; *Vivace*, quick and lively ; *Presto*, very quick.

Baroque sonatas were usually TRIO SONATAS, for two violins, viola da gamba (or cello) and harpsichord. They were called trios, in spite of the fact that they needed four players, because the music was written for only three parts. The viola da gamba's notes were practically identical with the lowest notes that were played on the harpsichord. The harpsichord, or CEMBALO part was not fully written out : only the bass notes were given, with numbers underneath them to show the player what chord to play. The numbers, or FIGURES, described the intervals above the bass note, such as $\frac{6}{3}$, $\frac{6}{4}$, $\frac{7}{3}$ etc., as in the examples in Parts V and VI. This kind of bass is called FIGURED BASS.

CHAPTER 34

CONTINUO

WHEN playing from a figured bass, a seventeenth-century harpsichord player had to IMPROVISE, or make up his own part, because the remaining notes had not been provided by the composer. As long as he kept to the harmonies that were indicated, he was free to space the chords in any way he liked, breaking them up into arpeggios, or embroidering them in the style of divisions.

The part played from a figured bass is called the CONTINUO, short for 'basso continuo', meaning 'continuous bass'. This somewhat puzzling name is a legacy from polyphonic music. At the end of the sixteenth century, composers were writing motets for twelve or more voices, and the singers needed the support of the organ. The organist was not given a special part of his own to play from, so he followed the voice parts, found out what vertical chords they were making, and then wrote in the figures such as $\frac{6}{3}$ or $\frac{7}{5}$ under the notes of the lowest bass singer's line of music. Every now and then the basses had several bars' rest, so the organist followed whichever was the lowest voice for the time being—perhaps a tenor, or even an alto—and wrote his figures under it, making a 'continuing bass' throughout the motet.

The English name for continuo is THOROUGH-BASS. ('Thorough' is the old word for 'through'.)

The working out of a keyboard part from the given figures is called the REALIZATION of the thorough-bass. (The word 'realize' is used in the sense of 'bringing into concrete existence'.)

With its imaginative variety of keyboard texture and its expressive support from viola da gamba or cello, a thorough-bass could provide the ideal accompaniment for the new style of seventeenth-century song which came into being as the result of the invention of OPERA.

CHAPTER 35

THE BEGINNINGS OF OPERA

IT was at the end of the sixteenth century that Italian poets and musicians made the first experiments in combining the two arts of drama and music. The poetic script, called the LIBRETTO, was specially written to be set to music. It was sung in a kind of musical speech called RECITATIVE, which followed the rhythm of the spoken words and the rise and fall of the spoken sentence.

The Italian composers very soon found that they needed to enrich the form of their works, or OPERAS, by introducing a more tuneful song, or ARIA, between the recitatives. The action of the drama was held up during the singing of an aria, while the singer stood still and sang either passionately, mournfully, cheerfully or triumphantly, according to the mood of that particular scene in the libretto. The words of an aria were not important in the unfolding of the plot, so the composer was free to repeat the same few words over and over again, in long-drawn-out phrases that might equally well have belonged to an instrumental work. Or he could repeat the same sentence, coming back to it again and again, like the refrain of a Rondeau. Or he could take one syllable of a word and make it last through half a dozen bars of rapid figuration—a style described as COLORATURA, because it coloured the outline of the tune.

The recitatives were used for getting on with the story, for conversations between the characters, for entries and exits, and for linking the arias to the rest of the scene. CHORUSES took an active part on the stage, often singing in quick contrapuntal imitation to represent the action of a crowd, or standing aside, like the chorus in Greek tragedy, and commenting on the drama in sustained harmony, as in Purcell's great opera, *Dido and Aeneas.*

Arias and recitatives had thorough-bass accompaniments. Choruses were accompanied by a group of instrumentalists called the ORCHESTRA. (The name ' orchestra ' was used for the first time in seventeenth-century opera : it is the Greek word for ' dancing-place '—the space between the stage and the auditorium in a Greek theatre which was kept for the dancers and instrumentalists.)

The seventeenth-century orchestra consisted of strings and harpsichord, with the occasional addition of recorders (which were called ' flutes '), oboes (which were no longer raucous), trumpets and drums.

There was no conductor : the harpsichord player directed the music from the keyboard. In an opera, the orchestra played an OVERTURE as an opening to the whole work—a short introduction in majestic, slow-moving chords with emphatic dotted rhythms, leading to a quick movement in fugal imitation. (The early overture was sometimes called a SYMPHONY, but the name had nothing to do with the symphonic form of the following centuries : it still had its earlier meaning of ' sounding together '.)

An instrumental interlude in a seventeenth-century opera was called a RITORNELLO, as it was like a refrain that commented on what had just been sung.

The orchestra played INCIDENTAL DANCES whenever they were needed, and between the acts there were ENTR'ACTES, or ACT TUNES, sometimes called CURTAIN TUNES, while the scene-shifters got the next scene ready.

Chapter 36

ORNAMENTS

One of the chief characteristics of all Baroque music, whether operatic or instrumental, was the lavish way that composers embellished their tunes. These embellishments were called Ornaments, or Grace-Notes.

Seventeenth-century performers usually improvised their own Gracing of a phrase, but later composers often showed what they wanted in written signs.

Grace-Notes are written much smaller than ordinary notes. They fit into the bar by taking time from the value of the note they are embellishing, without interfering with the pulse of the music :

An Appoggiatura ('leaning note') is a slow grace-note that leans on the main note it is embellishing, taking half the value of the note :

An appoggiatura before a dotted note takes two thirds of the value of that note :

An ACCIACCATURA (' crushed note ') is a quick grace-note that takes hardly any time at all : the main note follows it immediately.   It is written like an appoggiatura but with a stroke going through it :

written   **played**

(Appoggiaturas and acciaccaturas are always linked to the main note with a slur.   Their stems are written in the opposite direction to that of the main note.)

The word ORNAMENT is used for the various written signs for embellishments.   The most important ornaments are the MORDENT, the TURN and the TRILL (or SHAKE).

THE UPPER MORDENT :

THE LOWER MORDENT (or INVERTED MORDENT) :

THE TURN :

A turn between two notes :

A turn on or after a dotted note. (The last note of the turn equals the value of the dot) :

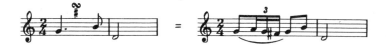

THE TRILL :

Ornaments vary according to the shape of the phrase and the speed at which it is to be sung or played. They also vary according to the century in which the music was written. No infallible rule can be given, but it is as well to remember that Baroque trills and turns *always begin on the upper note*. This tradition lasted right through the eighteenth century.

Part IX.   Style in the Early Eighteenth Century

CHAPTER 37

OPERA AND ORATORIO

CHANGES in STYLE in music have to be heard before they can be recognized, just as changes of style in clothes or architecture have to be seen rather than read about.   All that a text-book can do is to label some of the characteristic innovations that belong to each century.

The new operatic style in the first half of the eighteenth century was founded on the traditions of the opera-house in Naples.   In NEAPOLITAN OPERA the libretto and the music kept strictly to a conventional pattern.   Nearly every aria was in the form known as DA CAPO ARIA.   The words *da capo*, meaning ' from the beginning ', referred to the repetition of the whole of the first section after a contrasting second section had been sung.   The second section was in a different key, usually the relative minor.

The ARIA CANTABILE, or ' singing ' aria, needed a particular style of singing called BEL CANTO, in which beauty of sound was far more important than dramatic expression.

The ARIA DI BRAVURA had long, difficult passages in brilliant coloratura, with rapid runs, trills and florid ornaments : the performer who sang it was called a VIRTUOSO.

The ARIA DI CARATTERE, or *air de caractère*, was the only kind of song that had much to do with the story : it was essential that the words should be clearly heard, and there were places marked PARLANDO, ' as if speaking '.

Recitatives were either RECITATIVO STROMENTATO, accompanied by the orchestra, or RECITATIVO SECCO, accompanied by dry, abrupt chords from the harpsichord, like a succession of pin-pricks punctuating the rapidly sung conversations.

A Neapolitan opera consisted almost entirely of arias and recitatives, with only a few perfunctory choruses. The main characters never sang together in an ENSEMBLE, but kept to their allotted number of solos. The music was designed to allow for plenty of applause, and there was a strict rule that whoever was singing an aria must leave the stage immediately after the last note, so that he could be rapturously recalled by the audience. (This meant that when the hero proposed to the heroine he had to go off into the wings without waiting for her answer.) To compensate for the lack of dramatic characterization, producers spent fortunes on elaborate scenery and stage effects.

The greatest operatic composer at this time was Handel. His tunes had such vitality that they managed to bring life to the sawdust conventions of the opera houses. Handel's operas have seldom been performed since the eighteenth century, but the style of his operatic arias is familiar, owing to the many performances that are still given of his oratorios.

An eighteenth-century ORATORIO was an extended work, usually with a sacred libretto, written for performance in a church or a concert hall. After the earliest experiments, productions were without action, costumes or scenery. As in Neapolitan opera, the music consisted of recitatives and *da capo* arias, but there were many more opportunities for dramatic choruses, such as those in Handel's *Messiah*.

CHAPTER 38

BAROQUE CONCERTOS AND SONATAS

HANDEL'S orchestra was larger than Purcell's, but it was still directed from the harpsichord. Parts for the wind instruments were nearly always DOUBLED with the strings : the first and second oboes played the same notes as the first and second violins, and the bassoons played the same notes as the cellos. To vary the sound, there were passages for solo instruments alternating with the whole orchestra.

This was the texture of the early eighteenth-century CONCERTO, sometimes called CONCERTO GROSSO. The solo players were described as CONCERTINO, or PRINCIPALE ; the players who were not soloists were the TUTTI, or RIPIENO.

The form of Handel's concertos followed the tradition of the *sonata da chiese*, with four or more movements. Bach's solo concertos usually had only three movements : *Allegro, Adagio, Allegro*, which is the pattern that has remained ever since.

In a Handel Concerto Grosso the small group of *concertino* players very often consisted of two violins and continuo (harpsichord and cello), as in a Trio Sonata. The *ripieno* players were the rest of the strings, with the occasional addition of flutes, oboes, or trumpets.

The texture of Bach's *concerti grossi* (which are known by their title of ' Brandenburg concertos ') changed from one work to another. For instance, the second Brandenburg is written for the unexpected mixture of solo trumpet, flute, oboe, and violin, with the usual *tutti* of strings and continuo.

Concerti grossi are sometimes described as LATE BAROQUE CONCERTOS.

LATE BAROQUE SONATAS were mostly Trio Sonatas, but composers were also writing sonatas for one solo instrument and harpsichord. The chief difference between Handel's and Bach's sonatas for solo-with-harpsichord is that Handel was still writing his harpsichord parts as a figured continuo, to be realized by the player, whereas Bach was already giving his players a fully written-out part with a soloist's share of tunes for the right hand.

The form of the late Baroque sonata was like the *sonata da chiesa*, but occasionally one of the slow movements would be a dance such as the SICILIANO in Ex. 140 :

Ex. 140

Siciliano

Bach
(E♭ Sonata for Flute and Cembalo)

etc.

(This graceful dance, with its long flowing lines in dotted $\frac{6}{8}$ or $\frac{12}{8}$, is very similar to the $\frac{12}{8}$ PASTORALE, which is the form of the Pastoral Symphony in Handel's *Messiah*.)

Dances, however, were not often used in sonatas, as they belonged to the eighteenth-century equivalent of the *sonata da camera*, which was known as the SUITE.

CHAPTER 39

SUITES

THE early eighteenth-century SUITE was a short collection of contrasting dance tunes : it was called ' Suite ' because the tunes followed one after another. The Italian name for Suite is PARTITA. (Both languages are found side by side at this time, because France and Italy shared the supremacy in instrumental music.)

The movements of a Suite were not meant to be danced to : composers were free to lengthen the tunes when they wanted to.

The dances were all in the same key, with an occasional change to the tonic minor or major.   The *Allemande*, *Courante*, *Sarabande*, and *Gigue* were the essential movements, and they were played in that order : other dances could be added to them.   This was the pattern that Bach used in all his Suites, whether for orchestra or for solo instruments.

The ALLEMANDE had little in common with the Alman, for it was much slower and more graceful.   It was in a moderate ⁴₄, beginning with a short up-beat, and it usually had passing notes and rapidly flowing scales or arpeggios.

Ex. 141

There were two kinds of *Courante*.   The Italian CORRENTE was in quick ³₈ or ³₄, with continuous running figures : it was a direct descendant of the earlier dance (compare the sixteenth-century *Coranto* in Ex. 131, page 107):

Ex. 142

The French COURANTE was in fairly slow ³₂, with the rhythm sometimes hovering between ³₂ and ⁶₄:

Ex. 143

The SARABANDE was very much slower than the seventeenth-century dance. It kept the characteristic long note on the second beat:

Ex. 144   **Bach**
Sarabande   (English Suite No. IV)

Sarabandes were often played twice through, with elaborate embellishments at the repetition. Most early eighteenth-century players improvised their own embellishments. Bach was one of the first composers to write out the ornaments he wanted, which is why his printed music is apt to look more complicated than it really is.

The GIGUE, sharing some of the characteristics of the English Jig, was in quick compound time, often with leaping intervals suggesting a dancer's energetic steps :

Ex. 145   **Bach**
Gigue   (French Suite No. V)

The Gigue was always the last dance of the Suite. For the extra movement, which usually came between the Sarabande and the Gigue, there were at least a dozen other dances to choose from, including the Bourrée, Gavotte and Minuet. ('Minuet' was written the French way—Menuet—in Suites, and the Italian way—Minuetto—in Partitas.)

The BOURRÉE kept the simple character of the earlier Borry :

Ex. 146   **Bach**
Bourée I   (English Suite No. II)

A Bourrée was often followed by a second Bourrée in the tonic major or minor, with a *da capo* return to the first tune.

The GAVOTTE was in fairly quick $\frac{2}{2}$, with each phrase beginning half way through the bar :

Ex. 147

The major Gavotte No. 2 which follows this particular tune is a MUSETTE. This was the name of the seventeenth-century French bagpipes : the music imitates the sound of the DRONE with its long-drawn-out bass note :

Ex. 148

(A held bass note such as the drone in Ex. 148 is called a PEDAL, which is short for PEDAL POINT, the word ' point ' being used in its old meaning of ' note ', as in ' counterpoint '.)

The Minuet was still very similar to Purcell's Minuet, but in a Suite it had a quicker speed than when it was performed as a stately dance. It was always followed by a second minuet for three solo instruments (or, if the Suite was for harpsichord, in three-part harmony), with a *da capo* return. The second minuet was described as a ' Menuet en trio '. The name was soon shortened to TRIO.

Each movement in a Suite had a double bar half way through, with a modulation to the dominant. This was a real modulation, not a passing modulation. The tune had to be willing to turn back to the original tonic at the repeat, but it had to be equally willing at the second time bar to *go on in the new key*. In a Suite, where every dance is in the same key, it is essential to get away from that key during the course of each movement, so that the ear may welcome the home-coming at the final cadence.

The balanced form of the two halves of a dance movement is sometimes described as BINARY form. When two similar movements are linked with a *da capo* repetition the form is TERNARY.

Several of Bach's orchestral Suites are known as OUVERTURES. This seems confusing, but they are called this because their opening movement is in the form of the seventeenth-century French operatic overture, with a majestic introduction in dotted rhythm. The name 'Ouverture' was used for the opening movement of works for a solo instrument as well as for orchestra. It was a form of PRELUDE—a piece to be played before other movements.

Bach also used the name SINFONIA both in his orchestral music and in his harpsichord pieces. The word had nothing to do with what we think of as a symphony : it was just a name for an introductory instrumental piece.

Bach's Partitas and Suites for solo violin or solo cello without accompaniment need virtuoso players, for the texture of the single part has to carry not only the tune but also the harmonies that the tune has grown from. The harmonic foundation of Bach's music is so clear that it is always possible to recognize his chords, whatever the texture may be. In Ex. 149 the figuration looks elaborate, but there is nothing difficult about the harmony :

Ex. 149   **Bach**
(Cello Suite No. I)

Prelude

etc.

If the first three notes of each bar are played as chords, slowly, one after another, the music sounds as simple as a chorale.

CHAPTER 40

CANTATAS

CHORALES were the foundation of much of Bach's music. As organist of St. Thomas's Church, Leipzig, he not only harmonized chorales for the congregation to sing, but also wrote extended CANTATAS, founded on familiar chorale tunes, which were sung and played during the Sunday services.

A Bach CANTATA often begins with a chorus in which the sopranos sing the notes of a chorale in augmentation, supported by trumpets or oboes, while the other voices and instruments weave their counterpoint round it and the organ continuo reinforces the harmony. After the opening chorus, which is the longest section of the work, there are contrasted arias for solo voices with continuo accompaniment, sometimes linked by short recitatives, or ARIOSO sections, in a style half-way between an aria and a recitative. In many of the arias the solo voice is joined by a solo instrument that plays its own individual tune. This essential part for an instrument is called an OBLIGATO (or ' obbligato ' : the Oxford Dictionary gives both spellings). The cantatas always end with a straightforward version of the chorale, which, in Bach's time, could be sung by the congregation.

Members of the congregation would have known the chorale beforehand, since Bach always began the service by playing the tune as a voluntary on the organ, either as a CHORALE PRELUDE (sometimes called ORGAN CHORALE) or as CHORALE VARIATIONS, which followed the tradition of sixteenth-century Variations on a Theme.

Chorales are also the foundation of Bach's *Christmas Oratorio* (which is really six cantatas to be sung on different days), and of his Passion music.

The settings of the PASSION are extraordinarily ' operatic ' in the true sense of the word. The singers in the chorus represent the turbulent crowd, pushing their way to the front with each fugal entry ; or they stand aside from the action and comment on it in the expressive harmonies of the chorales. The Evangelist's recitatives set the imaginary stage for each change of scene, and every climax in the drama is followed by a contemplative aria with orchestral or obligato accompaniment.

The form of these extended works, and of the great *Mass in B minor*, is held together through all the changes of mood and texture by Bach's wonderful sense of key relationships.

CHAPTER 41

FUGUE

BACH was the first composer to write music in every possible key. His two sets of keyboard pieces in each of the twelve major and tonic minor keys are called the *Forty-Eight Preludes and Fugues*. The work has become so famous that it is often referred to as ' the Forty-Eight '. Bach's own name for it was *Das Wohltemperierte* (' well-tempered ') *Clavier*.

The word CLAVIER means ' keyboard ' : it applies to the clavichord as well as to the harpsichord.

The word ' well-tempered ' refers to Bach's system of tuning keyboard instruments. The earliest tuning of scales was founded on the notes of the harmonic series ; the size of each tone or semitone differed slightly. This was all right for music that consisted of a single line of melody, but when music was sung in contrapuntal intervals, some adjustment had to be made. The scale therefore became flexible, and singers altered the position of some of its degrees very slightly, in order to make the contrapuntal intervals sound in tune.

This instinctive process still goes on in unaccompanied choirs when singers listen to each other.   But the scale on a keyboard instrument cannot be flexible : it has to be modified, or ' tempered '.

JUST INTONATION, or ' true tuning ', which was founded on the intervals of the pure fifth and the pure third, gave the perfectly-in-tune triads of C—E—G, F—A—C, and G—B—D, but the other intervals were unsatisfactory.   In the sixteenth century the tuning was modified by making all the fifths slightly too small.   This MEAN-TONE system worked well for keys with only one or two sharps or flats, but in the late seventeenth and early eighteenth centuries, when music began modulating to remote keys, it became unusable.   There was such a difference in sound between G♯ and A♭ that if the A♭ were reasonably well tuned for the flat keys it could never be used as a G♯.   Organs and harpsichords were sometimes built with divided key-levers for G♯ and A♭, and for D♯ and E♭, in an attempt to get over this difficulty.

Our present system of tuning, called EQUAL TEMPERAMENT, divides the octave into twelve equal semitones, making every interval except the octave slightly out of tune.   (The tuner does not adjust the intervals by guessing how much out of tune they should be : he counts the acoustic beats mentioned on page 50, when tuning a keyboard instrument.)

This division of the octave spreads the discrepancy so evenly that it is possible to play in all keys.

Equal temperament was not in general use in Bach's life-time.   He was one of the pioneers, and the music he wrote made it essential for later musicians to change to the new method of tuning.

Bach's *Forty-Eight Preludes and Fugues* were not mere theoretical experiments : they were practical keyboard studies which he wrote as lessons for his children.   The preludes are in the form of ouvertures, toccatas, pastorales or concerto movements.   Several are in what is called DOUBLE COUNTER-POINT and TRIPLE COUNTERPOINT, which means that the bass can change places with the treble and still make sense, as in

Bach's two-part and three-part INVENTIONS.

The fugues in the Forty-Eight are for two, three, four, or five parts called 'voices'. (This word was still used for all eighteenth-century fugal counterpoint, even when the parts were instrumental.) The first voice comes in with the theme, or SUBJECT, which is short, and easily remembered owing to its distinctive rhythmic shape and its highly individual character. When the first voice gets to the end of the subject, the second voice enters in fugal imitation : this entry is called the ANSWER. Meanwhile the first voice goes on with the COUNTERSUBJECT, which is a new theme with an entirely different rhythm and shape. When the third voice enters with the subject, the second voice is given the countersubject.

The third voice need not come in immediately the second voice has finished the subject ; there can be a short EPISODE, where the first and second voices have small fragments of tunes called MOTIVES, which are often borrowed from the subject or countersubject. The voices toss these fragments from one to the other, or they repeat them, beginning on a different note each time, in SEQUENCE. When the last voice reaches the end of the subject, the EXPOSITION, or 'setting forth' is complete. (See p. 132.)

In a fugue, a subject beginning on the tonic is answered on the dominant. A subject beginning on the dominant is answered on the tonic. (This follows the Renaissance tradition mentioned in Chapter 17.) If the answering voice in a fugue is an exact transposition of the subject, the answer is described as REAL. The notes of the answer may have to be adjusted, to allow a subject moving from the tonic to the dominant to be answered by the dominant moving to the tonic, and vice versa, as in authentic and plagal entries in polyphony. An adjusted answer in a fugue is called a TONAL answer.

After the exposition, the fugal entries modulate to nearly-related keys, working their way back to the original key for the last entry. In order to celebrate this return to the tonic there is sometimes a CODA, or tail-piece, which prolongs the enjoyment of the home-coming.

During the working out of a fugue there is unexpected variety in the order in which the voices enter, and no voice ever returns to the subject at exactly the same level of pitch. (The later entries at the tonic or dominant are an octave higher or lower than before.) Sometimes the answering voice grows impatient while waiting for its turn, and comes in too soon, in an entry in STRETTO. And sometimes a voice pretends to be coming in with the subject, but changes its mind after the first few notes. This is called a FALSE ENTRY. In Ex. 150 the first voice has a false entry just before the true entry of the third voice:

Ex. 150

FUGUE for 3 voices

Bach
(Forty-eight Preludes and Fugues, Bk. I)

etc.

Other devices used by Bach in his fugal works and canons include AUGMENTATION of a subject, with the note values doubled, and DIMINUTION, with the note values halved. Bach not only INVERTED his subjects by turning their melodic intervals upside-down, but also used them backwards, or RETROGRADE, beginning with the last note and ending with the first one. (Other names for retrograde are CANCRIZANS, ' crab-wise ', and AL ROVESCIO, ' in reverse '.)

All these devices had been used in sixteenth-century polyphony. The difference between the early counterpoint and Bach's is that Bach always built his counterpoint on a foundation of silently-heard chords. For this reason it is sometimes described as HARMONIC COUNTERPOINT. In *The Art of Fugue*, written at the very end of his life, Bach went further than any other composer, before or since, in the miraculous interweaving of his fugal counterpoint.

Part X.   Late Eighteenth–Century Style

CHAPTER 42

MUSIC FOR ENTERTAINMENT

THE year 1750, when Bach died, marks the end of the Baroque period of music. Bach's style was already considered old-fashioned at the time of his death : two years later, musicians were talking about ' shaking off the useless fetters of counterpoint '.

During the last thirty years of Bach's life a great deal of the music that was being written throughout Europe was intended to be a form of entertainment. LIGHT OPERA was produced in every city that had an opera house. It was called by a different name in each different country. The OPERA BUFFA of Italy began as a series of short interludes performed between the acts of a serious opera. These interludes, called INTER-MEZZI, were often more successful than the main work, and were soon transformed into independent comic operas.

In France, the OPÉRA COMIQUE began as VAUDEVILLE, a dramatic entertainment of popular songs strung together with spoken dialogue. The German equivalent was the SINGSPIEL. The English equivalent was the BALLAD OPERA. The most famous example, *The Beggar's Opera*, had tunes from works by Purcell and Handel and from popular collections of English country dances. There was no virtuoso singing. The simple songs were satisfying in themselves and were sufficient for an evening's entertainment.

Instrumental music was also light and entertainingly ' pretty ' : Rococo is the name that is sometimes applied to it. There were short, descriptive pieces for harpsichord, such as Rameau's *La Poule*, where the rapid dry staccato imitates the clucking of the hen :

Ex. 151

In Couperin's *Le Moucheron* (Ex. 152) the little fly buzzes round and round the same two chords in a persistent way that would have been utterly out of place in counterpoint :

Ex. 152

It was not only in descriptive pieces that the harmony moved to and fro with such persistence. In Scarlatti's magnificent one-movement Sonatas, which he himself called ' Exercises ', there are whole sentences built on the foundation of tonic and dominant chords, in a manner that is typical of the

late eighteenth century.   And Telemann's harpsichord pieces
are in a very different language from the fugues that he had
been brought up on :

Ex. 153

Allégrement

Telemann

This example of the STYLE GALANT has several characteristics
of the new sonata form : the plain, direct harmonic structure
of the first half, which is built entirely on the 'primary'
triads of I, IV, and V ; the passing modulations immediately
after the double bar ; the subject inverted in the bass and used
in sequence ; and the return to the main key with the repetition
of the original subject.

This is the style in which Bach's sons wrote, extending the short *galant* pieces into works as long as the earlier Trio Sonatas:

Ex. 154

The orchestra that Bach's sons wrote for had two flutes ('transverse' flutes, not recorders), two oboes, two bassoons, two horns and strings. The tunes were nearly always given to the first violins. There was no more continuo to provide the accompaniment, so the figuration and broken chords which were once played on the harpsichord were now given to the second violins and violas. There was far less doubling of parts. The wind instruments supported the strings by providing a more solid foundation of chords. The brass no longer played the highest notes of the harmonic series but came down to the middle notes, which were admirably suited to the characteristic to-and-fro between tonic and dominant, as in Ex. 155 :

Ex. 155

Quick movements were played much faster than in Baroque music. The word PASSAGE was in danger of losing its normal

meaning of 'any short section of a work' because it was so often
used for a section needing brilliant technical display.   Rapid
scales and arpeggios rose with virtuoso energy, and rippling
broken chords were played TREMOLANDO, as fast as trills.   The
music was punctuated with frequent rests.   Dynamics changed
from one extreme to another with dramatic suddenness, and
an occasional unexpected silent bar, called a GENERAL PAUSE,
helped to emphasize the importance of a climax.

The first experiments in the new orchestral style were made
in the German town of Mannheim, and from 1750 onwards
Germany and Austria became the chief centres of instrumental
music.

CHAPTER 43

SONATA FORM

IT was from C. P. E. Bach and the Mannheim orchestra that
Haydn learnt to write in SONATA FORM.   This should really
be called ' first-movement-of-a-sonata form ', as the shape
need not apply to any of the other movements of a sonata.

Ex. 156 is the first movement of a Haydn SONATINA, or
' little sonata ', which has some of the characteristics of sonata
form although it is in miniature :

Ex. 156

Sonatina
Allegro moderato

Haydn

In a SONATA the FIRST SUBJECT, which is in the tonic, is followed by a short BRIDGE PASSAGE, like an episode, which modulates very deliberately to the dominant. This modulation, which is often emphasized by dynamics and rests, is followed by the SECOND SUBJECT, in the dominant. This is a contrasting tune : if the first subject has been firm and declamatory the second subject will probably be gentle and lyrical, or light and sparkling. The second subject leads to another emphatic assertion of the dominant cadence, often repeated several times, so that there can be no doubt in the listener's mind that the first section of the music is over. This first section is called the EXPOSITION. At the end of the exposition there is a double bar with repeat signs. After the double bar comes the DEVELOPMENT section, which uses fragments of the first and second subjects, tossing them about and combining them in a frequently-changing texture that moves in sequence from one passing modulation to the next, often borrowing contrapuntal devices such as inversion and diminution. There are seldom any new tunes in the development section. Economy is essential, for the listener has to be kept in a mood of suspense during the mounting excitement in which the music works up to its climax. The climax is the chord of the dominant, which arrives with unmistakable conviction after numerous passing modulations have hinted at other keys without ever becoming involved in them. This dominant chord is no longer the key-chord, as it was at the double bar : it now has the strong pull of a dominant seventh chord that is longing to resolve to the tonic. The actual resolution is the moment that the whole of the music has been leading up to : it is the beginning of the RECAPITULATION, when the first subject returns in its original tonic key. The recapitulation section has the same music as the exposition, but the second subject is in the tonic instead of the dominant. The emphatic assertion of the final tonic cadence is sometimes extended to a coda, which stresses the fact that the whole movement has come to an end.

A general outline of ' Sonata Form ' can never be satisfactory because there is no infallible map that can be followed from the first note to the last. Every sonata has its own individual characteristics, and the only way to study its form is to learn the sound of its music.

CHAPTER 44

QUARTETS, SYMPHONIES, AND CONCERTOS

SONATA form was not only used in sonatas. It was the form for all first movements of SYMPHONIES (which were like orchestral sonatas), and all concertos and CHAMBER MUSIC works. Chamber music groups played in rooms rather than in concert halls : they were the direct descendants of sixteenth-century consorts. In chamber music there were no more Trio Sonatas. The harpsichord, with its plucked strings, went out of fashion soon after Bach's death, and the new hammer-action keyboard instrument was the FORTEPIANO, the ancestor of our piano. It was called this because it could play both loudly and softly within one short phrase. The harpsichord could play f or p, but it was not able to provide the new dynamic of ⊂ ⊃.The fortepiano could sustain the sound of its notes longer than the harpsichord, and it was therefore able to do without the support of a stringed instrument doubling the bass notes. Thorough-bass was no longer needed : in the new sonatas for violin and fortepiano the two instrumentalists were equal partners.

The most important of the new chamber music ensembles was the STRING QUARTET : first violin, second violin, viola, and cello. Haydn's earliest experimental string quartets were in the same form as the late eighteenth-century works for string orchestra, such as the DIVERTIMENTO (in French, DIVERTISSE-MENT), which was a collection of short movements, some of them like Trio Sonata movements, others like dances from Suites ; the CASSATION, an out-of-doors Divertimento ; and the SERENADE and NOTTURNO, which were Cassations for the late evening.

Haydn was able to try out as many experiments as he liked with his own group of players in Prince Esterházy's palace, and he soon found that he needed a more intimate form than the Divertimento to suit the texture of his new ensemble. The four string players sat facing inwards. In this position they were able to listen intently to each other, and could enjoy instrumental conversations with subtle arguments and asides. In exchanging their musical ideas they were able to express an infinite variety of moods, while keeping to the courteous formality of late eighteenth-century manners.

Eighteenth-century string quartets and symphonies had four movements. Sonatas and concertos had three movements. The first movement was nearly always quick. The second movement, which was slow, could also be in sonata form, or it could be a theme and variations, or a movement in the form of a *da capo* aria, or a simple tune like a song. String quartets and symphonies had a Minuet and Trio between the slow movement and the last movement. This was the only dance movement that survived in instrumental music in the late eighteenth century. The Trio was no longer for three instruments, but its texture was always lighter than that of the Minuet.

The last movement, or FINALE, was nearly always the quickest movement. Often it was a RONDO, with the first section repeated after each new section, as in the seventeenth-century Rondeau.

Concertos were no longer written for *concertino* and *ripieno* instruments. There were occasional DOUBLE or TRIPLE CONCERTOS, for two or three soloists, but mostly they were written for one solo string or wind instrument, or for forte-piano, with orchestral accompaniment. The tunes on which the movements were founded were often characteristic of the particular solo instrument, as in Ex. 157, which is the beginning of the Finale of a Horn concerto in the typical six-eight rhythm of a hunting song :

Ex. 157

Rondo from Horn Concerto K. 495
Allegro vivace
Mozart
etc.

Many of Mozart's symphonies and concertos were written for the same small orchestra that Bach's sons wrote for. Others were for a larger orchestra including clarinets, trumpets, and drums. In concertos the texture of the orchestra was much lighter for the passages where the soloist was playing : when the soloist stopped playing, the passages for full orchestra were described as ' tutti '.

Soloists had to be virtuoso players. The brilliant scales and arpeggios in the music were much quicker than in the earlier *concerti grossi,* and the tone had to be more penetrating to contend with the greater volume of sound in the orchestral accompaniment. At the soloist's final cadence there was a pause at the cadential $^6_4$ chord while the orchestra waited in silence for the player to grace the resolution in an *ad libitum* passage called a CADENZA.

CHAPTER 45

CLASSICAL VIENNESE CHURCH MUSIC
AND OPERA

THE end of the eighteenth century is often called the period of VIENNESE CLASSICAL MUSIC. This is because the geniuses Haydn and Mozart were living in Vienna and were designing their music with that sense of balance which we describe as ' classical '.

They wrote not only symphonies and concertos and quartets and sonatas, but also church music and operas. Haydn's oratorios follow the tradition of Handel—he wrote his *Creation* after hearing a London performance of *Messiah*. But his Masses have nothing in common with the masterpieces of Renaissance counterpoint. The polyphonic tradition had died out, and late eighteenth-century composers were so out of touch with music for unaccompanied voices that when Mozart was a child his teachers made him learn ' strict ' counterpoint out of a text-book—the same kind of ' Five Species ' counterpoint that is still taught for examination purposes.

Mozart's own Masses are in the expressive classical style of the accompanied arias, ensembles, and choruses of his operas. It was in opera that he felt most at home. Fortunately for him, the narrow operatic conventions of the early eighteenth century had been done away with. Gluck had brought a ' beautiful simplicity ' to the operatic stage. There was not so much virtuoso display of technique ; songs were simpler, and dramatic expression was again true instead of false. When Mozart wrote his Italian operas he was free to introduce comedy into his tragedies and tragedy into his comedies, and he could give each of his characters a musical personality. His German operas were founded on the ' Singspiel ', but they were immensely greater than any that had been written before.

In *The Magic Flute* the music is as deeply expressive as in the greatest of his instrumental works. Every tune has an unmistakable ' rightness ', and the rise and fall of each sentence, as in Ex. 158, is perfectly balanced :

Ex. 158

This balance of form in classical eighteenth-century music can be recognized as clearly as in eighteenth-century architecture, and the recognition brings a lasting sense of satisfaction.

Part XI. Nineteenth-Century Music

CHAPTER 46

THE CHANGE OF STYLE FROM CLASSICAL TO ROMANTIC

BY the beginning of the nineteenth century a classical perfection of balance was no longer the ideal to be followed : its place was taken by a very different kind of vitality. This was chiefly owing to Beethoven, a genius whose vehement personality prompted him to shatter the poised control of the late eighteenth century.

Beethoven's name is often included among the Viennese classical composers, because he was working in Vienna when Haydn was still alive. But the difference in the style of their music can be heard as early as in Beethoven's first symphony. Haydn's orchestral Minuets, though they were too quick to be danced to, still bore a faint resemblance to the movement from the eighteenth-century Suite. But in Ex. 159 the tune of Beethoven's new sort of Minuet rushes uphill with an impetuous abandon :

Ex. 159

Menuetto

Allegro molto e vivace

Beethoven
(From Symphony No. 1)

Soon after Beethoven had written this tune the word 'Minuet' was discarded, and the symphonic movement was renamed SCHERZO : its $\frac{3}{4}$ time signature was transformed into one-in-a-bar.

The change in the style of first-movement sonata form was even more startling. The eighteenth-century scaffolding remained, with its outline of first subject, second subject, development and recapitulation. But a first subject was seldom content with an economical statement of tonic-and-dominant : it was more likely to become a violently passionate protest, hurled, as it were, at the listener's head. With so much emotional excitement packed into the opening bars, it was inevitable that the development section should cease to be a meeting-place for courteous conversation, and should turn into a battle-ground where every gesture could lead to a tremendous upheaval.

Courteous formality was a thing of the past. The elegant eighteenth-century dances had disappeared with the wig, and nineteenth-century ballroom enthusiasts began by borrowing cheerful peasant dances such as the LÄNDLER. (In Ex. 160 the time-pattern is stressed with Beethoven's favourite dynamic, the sforzando.)

Ex. 160

The energetic Ländler soon developed into the graceful WALTZ, which was the most popular of all dances throughout the whole century. In a Waltz, the accompaniment to the four-bar or eight-bar phrases has one consonance or dissonance throughout each bar : the texture nearly always consists of a bass note on the first crotchet with repeated chords on the second and third, as in Ex. 161 :

Ex. 161
Waltz   Schubert

The chromatic harmonies in the Viennese Waltz in Ex. 161, with their warmth and lyrical persuasiveness, are typical of romantic nineteenth-century music at its very best. And the enharmonic fluctuations are particularly characteristic of Schubert. His cadences can hint at distant keys without losing their sense of direction.

It is not only in his Waltzes that Schubert manages to say so much in a few short bars : his songs, called LIEDER, are miracles of economy. The tunes are as simple as folk songs, yet every subtle mood in the poems is perfectly expressed in the music.

The word LIED, which is the German for ' song ', is used for a particular kind of song with piano accompaniment. Schubert was the first to write these new songs with equal partnership for singer and pianist. He also invented the form of the SONG CYCLE, a collection of separate songs linked together to make a complete work.

Chapter 47

DESCRIPTIVE MUSIC

THE equal partnership between singer and player in Schubert's songs was helped by the subtleties of touch and tone in the new nineteenth-century piano. This instrument was mellower than the eighteenth-century fortepiano. It was also much more powerful, and had more variety of dynamic expression.

Schumann was one of the first of the many nineteenth-century composers of piano music to become passionately interested in the technical possibilities of the instrument. Ex. 162 is real piano music, with its singing tone in the right hand and its legato broken chords in the left:

Ex. 162

Erinnerung ('Reminiscence')   Schumann
Not fast and to be played with a singing tone

etc.

Ex. 162 is one of Schumann's many short pieces with descriptive titles. These CHARACTER PIECES were distantly related to the eighteenth-century descriptive pieces, but in the nineteenth century they expressed a more personal emotion and were given titles such as ' Dreaming ', ' First Loss ', or ' The Poor Orphan '. Other more general titles used by Schumann and the pianist-composers Chopin, Mendelssohn, Brahms, and Liszt include SONGS WITHOUT WORDS, with a singable tune in the right hand ; MOMENT MUSICAL, a short lyrical piece ; IMPROMPTU, an impulsive piece (not an improvisation) ; BAGATELLE, a light-hearted piece (from the French for ' trifle ') ; CAPRICCIO and HUMORESQUE, capricious pieces with frequent changes of mood ; NOCTURNE, a slow dreamlike piece, often with a melancholy tune over a broken-chord accompaniment ; NOVELETTE, an eventful piece with a story to it ; BALLADE, a dramatic (or melodramatic) piece with a lyrical middle section. A FANTASIA was not contrapuntal, as in the sixteenth century : it was a fantastic or dreamlike piece. A RHAPSODY was as free as a Fantasia and could be as heroically dramatic as a Ballade. The name SCHERZO, having nothing to do with a symphonic scherzo, was used for a piece in Ballade form. The words PRELUDE and INTERMEZZO lost their original meaning in nineteenth-century piano music : Preludes were written with nothing to follow them, and Intermezzi with nothing on either side of them.

There were also descriptive works for orchestra. A concert piece called an OVERTURE could be independent of any opera. Mendelssohn's *Midsummer Night's Dream Overture* was written as in introduction to the spoken play, but his *Hebrides Overture* was a self-contained orchestral work.

SYMPHONIC POEMS or TONE POEMS were one-movement orchestral works based on a descriptive idea.

Instrumental music that tells a story or describes a scene in nature is called PROGRAMME MUSIC. Many nineteenth-century composers preferred to write a character piece rather than a sonata, or a symphonic poem rather than a symphony, because the style of programme music was more in keeping with the

ROMANTICISM of the time.

The word ROMANTIC is defined in the dictionary as 'imaginative' and 'passionate', but these are qualities that belong to all great music af any generation. Nineteenth-century romantic music is different from eighteenth-century classical music in its form and texture, as well as in its idiom. It began under the influence of a group of German poets and novelists who tried to escape from the ordinary everyday world into an imaginary world of their own.

As a result of this influence, composers broke away from the everyday eighteenth-century task of writing music to order, preferring to write music that expressed their own personal feelings. Each composer brought his own individual contri-bution to the romanticism of his time.

One of the chief characteristics of the romantic style is a love of CHROMATICISM. Chromatic scales are very easy to play on the piano, and before long the pianist-composers were indulging in highly-coloured passages in which every available half-inch was filled with chromatic chords, as in Ex. 163 :

In orchestral music chromaticism led to a change in the construction of brass instruments, and by the middle of the century horns and trumpets were no longer limited to the notes of the harmonic series, but could play chromatic cres-cendos at an approach to a climax. Chromatic passages for the brass did more than anything else to keep up the emotional tension during the long acts of nineteenth-century opera.

Chapter 48

ROMANTIC OPERA, MUSIC-DRAMA, AND BALLET

German Romantic Opera began with the scenes of magic and horror in Weber's *Der Freischütz*. Romantic librettos were based on legends from German history or folk-lore. Witches, monsters and thunderstorms played an important part in the unfolding of the drama, and the story often roused feelings of patriotism in the audience.

Wagner was the most adventurous of the nineteenth-century German operatic composers : by the middle of the century he was no longer satisfied with the pattern of romantic opera, and he began working out his own theory of opera as Music-Drama, in which all the arts were to combine in a new form. The music was no longer to be divided into arias and recitatives. The words, which were to be sung in a free rhythm, were concerned with the ' outer action ' of events, while the orchestra was to provide the feelings, or ' inner action ', of the drama. The orchestral music was to be continuous throughout each act, with no double bars to suggest that a section had come to an end, and no perfect cadence to suggest that a full stop had been reached.

Wagnerian acts were long, and the timing was planned on a vast scale. The orchestra was larger and more powerful than it had ever been before, and singers had to contend with the sustained resonance and vigorous outbursts of their ' accompaniment '. The form of the music was held together by the use of the Leitmotiv, or ' leading motive ', which was a short basic theme representing a certain character, or situation, or symbolic idea.

The most famous of all Wagner's leading motives, from the opening of *Tristan und Isolde*, is characteristic of the intensity of emotion in his harmony, with its piled-up sequences and its long-drawn-out chromatic passing-notes :

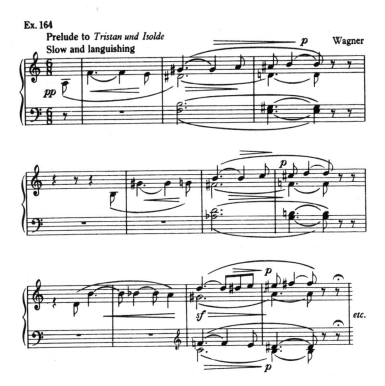

Ex. 164
Prelude to *Tristan und Isolde*
Slow and languishing
Wagner

There is nothing new about the interval of the augmented sixth in the second bar of Ex. 164 : Bach had used it more than a hundred years before this in his congregational hymn tunes. With Bach, however, it led to the resolution of a perfect cadence, whereas in Ex. 164 it leads to an unsatisfied, unresolved dominant seventh.

The UNRESOLVED DISCORDS in Wagner's music, and his so-called 'endless melody' influenced many of the late nineteenth-century composers and led them to abandon their previous ideas about form in music.   But there were those who never came under his spell.   Verdi continued to write superb operas without any leading motives or unresolved discords in them, and although at the end of his life he turned aside from the 'operatic numbers' that were a legacy from the old Neapolitan conventions, he kept the glory of *bel canto* alive in his beautiful tunes.

Tchaikovsky was another composer who was uninfluenced by leading motives : his operas and ballets, written at the end of the century, had tunes that were as definite in their shape as Mozart's arias.

Nineteenth-century BALLET could never have existed without clearly-defined tunes, for it was founded on a pattern of set pieces such as the PAS DE DEUX, PAS DE SIX and PAS D'ACTION.   The terms used in ballet are always in French, because the earliest ballets came from France.   The CHOREO-GRAPHERS who make up the steps and figures of the dances use several Italian musical terms but they give them different meanings ;   for instance, 'Adagio' is the name of the slow pas-de-deux for the leading ballerina and her partner at the climax of the ballet, and 'Allegro' is used for the quick turns and leaps that are performed 'in the air'.   The word 'Variation' is not used in its musical sense : it is the term for a solo dance in a ballet.

In nineteenth-century ballet some of the set pieces, or 'numbers', were NATIONAL DANCES of Spain or Hungary or Russia, but although they were founded on folk tunes there was nothing primitive about their musical settings. When Tchaikovsky introduced a Russian 'Trepak' into his *Nutcracker* or a Hungarian 'Czardas' into his *Swan Lake* he used all the resources of the full orchestra.

Part XII. The Full Orchestra of Today

Chapter 49

WOODWIND

The four main groups of instruments in a Full Orchestra are the Woodwind, Brass, Percussion, and Strings. They are written in that order in the Full Score, beginning at the top of the page with the highest woodwind instrument, and going down the page to the lowest string instrument.

The normal Woodwind Section of a full orchestra consists of two flutes and piccolo, two oboes and English horn, two clarinets and bass clarinet, and two bassoons and double bassoon.

(In the following details about the compass of these instruments the highest note possible is given. But these extreme notes are very seldom played. The usual compass reaches to about a fourth below the top note.)

The Flute has a compass from *c'* (or *b♭*) to *c''''*. In its lowest octave the notes are not very clear: they become brighter and more penetrating the higher they go.

The Piccolo, or ' little flute ', has a sounding compass from *d''* to *c'''''*. The piccolo part is written an octave lower than it sounds, to avoid having too many leger lines. The piccolo's high notes are very shrill and piercing.

The Alto Flute, which used to be called the Bass Flute, is occasionally used in orchestras. It has *g* as its lowest note. Its part is written a fourth higher than it sounds : this is to enable the player to change from the ordinary flute to the alto flute without having to learn a different fingering for the notes.

Instruments which have their parts written at a different level of pitch from the sound of the notes are called TRANSPOSING INSTRUMENTS. Players of transposing instruments refer to the *sound* of their written notes as CONCERT PITCH. (For example, the alto flute's written *c'* is ' concert *g* '.)

The OBOE has a compass from *b♭* to *g'''*. Its reedy quality, which is beautifully expressive in the middle range, becomes thin at the highest notes. The lowest notes are difficult to play softly. The old way of spelling the name is HAUTBOY, from the French *hautbois*.

The alto oboe is called the ENGLISH HORN or the COR ANGLAIS. (It may have got its name from the eighteenth-century *oboe da caccia*, ' hunting oboe ', which was curved in shape and looked something like an English hunting-horn.) The compass of the English horn is a fifth below that of the oboe. The English horn is a transposing instrument : it is written a fifth higher than it sounds, to enable an oboe player to change from one instrument to the other.

The CLARINET owes its name to the high ' clarino ' trumpet parts of the early eighteenth century. It is made in two sizes ; the one that is slightly longer has a compass a semitone lower than the other. Clarinet players always have both instruments with them when they are going to play, so that they can change from one to the other according to what key the music is in. Both instruments are transposing. The shorter is the CLARINET IN B♭ : its written *c'* sounds a tone lower (*b♭*). The longer instrument is the CLARINET IN A : its written *c'* sounds a tone and a half lower (*a*). The *written* compass of both clarinets is *e* to *a'''*. The tone of the lowest octave, known as the CHALUMEAU, can sound gloomy or mysterious. The two higher octaves have a clear tone that can be brilliant or mellow according to the mood and dynamics of the music. The very highest notes are shrill and need the support of an orchestral tutti.

The BASS CLARINET IN B♭ is written as if for ordinary B♭

clarinet but it sounds an octave lower.   The low notes of all
clarinets are written in the treble clef, although this may
involve using a great many leger lines.

There is a small, high clarinet with a compass sounding a
fourth higher than the B♭ clarinet.   It is the CLARINET IN
E♭, which is occasionally used in very large orchestras.   (Its
real home is the MILITARY BAND, where it is one of the most
important instruments.)   The E♭ clarinet's written *c'* sounds
a minor third higher (*e♭'*).

The BASSOON (in Italian, *Fagotto*) is the bass of the oboe
family.   Its compass is from B♭, to *d''*.   Its lowest notes are
rich and resonant : they are impossible to play swiftly or softly.
Its highest notes are thin : if played staccato they can sound
agile and light-hearted ; if played legato they can sound sad
and unearthly.   The bassoon part is written in the bass clef,
with a change to the tenor clef for the higher notes.

The DOUBLE BASSOON (Contrafagotto) has a compass an
octave lower than the bassoon.   The part is written an octave
higher than it sounds.

CHAPTER 50

BRASS

THE normal BRASS SECTION of an orchestra consists of four
horns, two or three trumpets, three trombones, and tuba.

The HORN is a transposing instrument.   It is nearly always in
F, with written *c'* sounding a fifth lower.   The OPEN NOTES
of the horn are the notes of the harmonic series.   Before the
nineteenth century, horn players found the other notes of the

scale by putting a hand inside the bell-shaped opening of the instrument and half-stopping the sound coming out. This altered the pitch of the note. But these STOPPED NOTES were not very satisfactory because the tone was weak. In the late eighteenth century an extra bit of tube called a CROOK could be fitted into the horn to alter the pitch of the harmonic series to any key that the music was in. This suited Haydn and Mozart, but the chromatically-minded composers of the nineteenth century were not satisfied. Instrument makers therefore added VALVES. These were short pieces of tube which could temporarily lower the pitch of any note. They made it possible for the horn to play a chromatic scale with the compass of written $F\sharp$ to c'''. Orchestral horns play in pairs : if there are four horns, I and III take the higher notes and II and IV the lower. Their parts are written in the treble clef. The very low notes are written in the bass clef, at the octave in which they are to sound. (In music written earlier than the middle of the nineteenth century these low notes were written an octave too low.)

TRUMPETS are higher instruments than horns and their shape gives them a more brilliant and piercing tone. Trumpets are in B♭, C, or D. Of the three, the B♭ is the most generally used. In early music trumpet parts were written in C, to be transposed if necessary. Today trumpet parts are written at concert pitch. With the help of valves, the harmonic series gives the trumpet a compass of $f\sharp$ to c'''. The part is written in the treble clef.

In full scores the trumpets are written below the horns, although they are higher in pitch. This is because the mellow tone of the horns can blend so well with the woodwind instruments that composers often allow the horns to share the texture of the bassoons and clarinets. Trumpets, being brassier, belong more to the trombones.

The three TROMBONES are divided into first and second TENOR TROMBONES and BASS TROMBONE. Like all brass instruments, the trombone has the natural open notes of the harmonic series. Long before valves were invented, the trombone was able to play the remaining notes with the help of a separate piece of tube called the SLIDE which can be moved in or out while playing.

The compass of the TENOR TROMBONE is from E to $b\flat'$. The first and second tenor trombones share a stave in a full score.   They are written in the tenor clef or bass clef, according to the range of the notes.

The BASS TROMBONE has a compass a fourth lower than the tenor trombone.   It is written in the bass clef.   In a full score it often has to share a stave with the TUBA.   This is an unsatisfactory arrangement, because the tuba is a very different instrument : its tone, which is mellow and cushiony, is much more like the horn.

The tuba should really be called the BASS TUBA, because there are other tubas of different sizes in BRASS BANDS.   The orchestral bass tuba, which is valved, has a compass from $D,$ to $a\flat'$.   It is written in the bass clef, with 8va..: for the lowest notes.

CHAPTER 51

PERCUSSION, CELESTA AND HARP

THE most important instrument in the PERCUSSION SECTION is the set of TIMPANI, or kettledrums.   A single kettledrum is hardly ever used.   Seventeenth and eighteenth-century composers used two timpani of different sizes, one tuned to the tonic and the other to the dominant.   (They could be tuned to any key, for a timpani player can alter the pitch of his instruments by loosening or tightening the skin or ' head ' of the drum.)   In the middle of the nineteenth century a third drum was added.   By the end of the century composers were asking for as many as six. A mechanical device was then invented for altering the pitch of a drum by a controlling pedal. It is these mechanically controlled CHROMATIC TIMPANI that are used today for any music that needs rapid changes of tuning. Timpani sticks have felt-covered heads that make it possible for the sound to vary from the *ff* of a thunderstorm to the *pp* of a distant murmur. Timpani parts are written in the bass clef. They are now given key signatures.

Other percussion instruments with a definite pitch are the GLOCKENSPIEL, an instrument like a primitive keyboard with steel notes struck with wooden hammers, and a compass from *c''* to *c'''''* which is written two octaves lower than it sounds, and the XYLOPHONE, a wooden glockenspiel with a compass from *c'* to *c'''''* which is written as it sounds.

TUBULAR BELLS are metal tubes hung from a frame and hit with a hammer. They are designed to imitate the sound of church bells : their usual compass is from *c'* to *f''*. They are described as having 'definite pitch', and their fundamental notes are carefully tuned, but the actual sound that reaches the ear is a conglomeration of 'extra' notes. This is because tubular bells, like church bells, are rich in audible overtones. They are so resonant that they go on sounding long after they have been struck. If two bells are played one after another the sound-waves pile up and produce RESULTANT NOTES. (There are two kinds of resultant note ; one is the SUMMATIONAL NOTE, which has a frequency equal to the sum of the frequencies of the original two notes ; the other is the DIFFERENTIAL NOTE, with a frequency equal to the difference between the frequencies of the two notes.)

Percussion instruments without any definite pitch have no need for a stave, so they are written on a single line. The most important of the indefinitely pitched percussion instruments is the SIDE DRUM. It can have a brilliant, exhilarating influence on the dynamics of a work, with its brittle accents and its rapid roll which can swell from *pp* to *ff* in the space of a bar.

The TAMBOURINE has a jingling sound that can mark the rhythm of a dance or quiver in a tremolo of excitement.

The TRIANGLE has a high-pitched, metallic insistence in its voice which can make itself heard through almost any orchestral tutti.

The CYMBALS are played by clashing one against the other, which can produce a terrifying clamour, or by suspending one cymbal and touching it *tremolando* with soft felt-headed timpani sticks, which can give a cloudy and mysterious effect.

The BASS DRUM (in Italian *gran cassa*) is played with a large soft-headed stick, and the deep thud of its voice can be awe-inspiring.

The GONG is even more ominous.   Its fortissimo can drown all other instruments (except for the shriek of the piccolo's top notes).   If played too loudly, beyond the ' threshold of pain ', it could damage the ears of the player, or of anyone else who was too near.

In a full score, the timpani is written on the highest stave belonging to the percussion section.   Next come the indefinitely pitched instruments on their single lines, and below them the ' keyboard ' percussion (Glockenspiel and Xylophone).

The CELESTA does not belong to the true percussion section : it is treated as an individual member of the orchestra.   It is like a very small piano, with a compass from c' to c''''', written an octave lower than it sounds.

The HARP is also an individual instrument in the orchestra. Its part is written in the full score between the celesta and the normal orchestral strings.   The harp has a string for each of the seven notes of the diatonic major scale throughout six and a half octaves.   It is tuned to the scale of C♭ major, with a compass from $C♭_{,}$ to $g♭''''$.   It has seven pedals which control each of the seven notes at every octave : with a single movement of the foot all C♭s are raised to C♮ ; at a second movement they are raised another semitone to C♯.   This ' double action ' adjustment makes it possible to play in any major or minor key.

By sliding the hands across all the strings the harpist can play scales much more rapidly than by the normal method of plucking.   This sliding is called GLISSANDO.   With the help

of enharmonic tuning it is possible to play glissando chords :
for instance, the diminished seventh chord on C can be
produced by tuning the seven strings to C D♯ E♭ F♯ G♭
A and B♯. Other possible glissando passages include the
WHOLE-TONE SCALE, which has no semitones in it. This scale
is difficult to sing or to play on an instrument where each
note has to be ' found ', for we usually depend on a mixture of
tones and semitones for our sense of relative pitch. But the
harp, with its enharmonic tuning, can easily play C D E
F♯ G♯ A♭ B♭.

The harp part is written like piano music on two staves
bracketed together.   Treble and bass clefs are used according to
the range of the notes.

If a piano or an organ is to be played in an orchestral work,
the parts are written below the harp part in the full score.

CHAPTER 52

STRINGS

The normal STRING SECTION of the orchestra can be used when
wanted as a complete STRING ORCHESTRA. It consists of
FIRST VIOLINS, SECOND VIOLINS, VIOLAS, CELLOS and DOUBLE
BASSES. The strings are the only section of the orchestra
where there are many players to one part. Composers
occasionally give the leading violinist, violist, cellist or double
bass player a solo passage, but most of the time they play in
unison with the other members of their group, sitting in
couples and sharing a music stand, or DESK.

The FIRST and SECOND VIOLINS both play the same sized

instrument, with the four open strings tuned *g d' a' e''* and a
compass of fingered or STOPPED NOTES from *g♯* to as high
as—or higher than—the human ear can hear.   The first
violins nearly always play a higher part than the second violins.
The leading first violin is called the LEADER of the whole
orchestra.   This name is a relic of the late eighteenth century
when the orchestra was conducted by the principal first violin.
Before that, the harpsichord player was the conductor.   It is
only since the early nineteenth century that a CONDUCTOR has
relied on a stick or BATON instead of an instrument.   And it is
only since the late nineteenth century that he has become an
authoritarian virtuoso.   The leading first violinist, however,
continues to be a leader in a very real sense of the word, for he
can help to create a flexibly responsive ensemble from a large
crowd of hard-worked individuals.   And, if the conductor is
inexperienced, the leader can unobtrusively carry on the
eighteenth-century tradition by encouraging the other members
of the orchestra to watch the point of his bow at every pause
or change of tempo.

The VIOLA is a larger instrument than the violin.   Its four
strings are tuned *c g d' a'*.   It is written in the alto clef, with
the treble clef for high notes.   Orchestral parts seldom go
much higher than *c'''* except in passages that are in unison or
octaves with the other strings.

The CELLO is a very much larger instrument than the viola.
Its full name is VIOLONCELLO.   The abbreviation was originally
written 'cello, with 'celli as the plural ; it is now written
without the apostrophe, and the plural is cellos.   The four
strings are tuned an octave lower than the viola.   The part is
written in the bass clef, with the tenor clef for the moderately
high notes, and the treble clef for the very high notes, which can
go up to *g''* or occasionally even higher.

The DOUBLE BASS (in Italian, CONTRABASSO) is so large that
its open strings have to be tuned in fourths because the stopped
notes are so far apart.   The four strings are tuned to *E, A, D G.*
The part is written in the bass clef, an octave higher than it
sounds.

The number of string players in a full orchestra depends on the balance of wind and percussion in the ORCHESTRATION. For a programme needing a large orchestra the proportion of strings could be twenty first violins, eighteen second violins, fourteen violas, twelve cellos and eight double basses.

The size of a full orchestra can vary considerably. Late nineteenth-century composers sometimes wrote for as many as four flutes and piccolo, four oboes and English horn, four clarinets and bass clarinet, four bassoons and double bassoon, eight horns, four trumpets, four trombones, tuba, timpani, percussion, two harps, piano, organ and strings. No orchestra since then has been any larger than this.

CHAPTER 53

ITALIAN TERMS AND ABBREVIATIONS USED IN SCORE-READING

IN trying to follow orchestral music from a MINIATURE SCORE, learners are often puzzled by unfamiliar Italian terms and signs and abbreviations. These all have their practical uses. Musicians consider Italian to be a kind of international language that enables instrumentalists in any country to play from the same ORCHESTRAL PARTS. Signs and abbreviations save labour as well as space, and they make the written appearance of the music easier to read.

The following list is a continuation of the terms and signs already mentioned on pages 42 to 45, and 117 to 119. Most of them are found not only in orchestral music but also in songs, instrumental solos, chamber music, PIANO REDUCTIONS of orchestral works and VOCAL SCORES (i.e., voice parts with piano reduction) of operas and choral works.

SOME OF THE TERMS USED FOR SPEED. (See also p. 42.)

Allargando : broadening out.

Calando ; gradually slower (and softer).

Doppio movimento ; double the speed (twice as fast).

L'istesso tempo ; the same speed (i.e., the beat remains the same at a change of time signature).

Meno mosso ; less movement (a slower speed).

Moderato ; at a moderate pace.

Più mosso ; more movement (a quicker speed).

Rubato ; lit. ' robbed ', meaning ' take your time ; not too strictly '.

Stringendo ; gradually faster.

Tempo giusto ; in strict time.

SOME OF THE TERMS FOR MOOD AND EXPRESSION. (See also p. 113 for speed indications which can also imply a mood.)

Agitato ; agitated.

Allegro ; quick and cheerful.

Allegretto ; not as fast as Allegro.

Andante ; gently moving.

Andantino ; slightly quicker than Andante.

Animato ; animated.

Cantabile ; singing tone.

Dolce ; sweetly.

Espressivo ; expressive.

Giocoso ; gaily.

Grazioso ; gracefully.

Largamente ; broadly.

Leggiero ; lightly.

Lento doloroso ; slowly and sadly.

Maestoso ; majestically.

Morendo ; dying away.

Pesante ; heavily.

Risoluto ; boldly.

Semplice ; simply.

Sostenuto ; sustained.

Tranquillo ; calm.

SOME OF THE WORDS FREQUENTLY USED IN DIRECTIONS TO PERFORMERS.

Assai ; very (e.g. Allegro assai).

Attacca ; go on at once to the next movement. (*Segue*, meaning ' it follows on ', is also used.)

Col or *colla* ; with the (e.g. *colla voce*—keep with the voice while accompanying a singer's rubato.)

Come ; as (e.g. *come prima*—as at first, after a contrasting section).

Con ; with (e.g. *con sordino*—with the mute, a device for softening the tone of an instrument).

Ma ; but (e.g. *ma non troppo*—but not too much, after a direction such as accel. or rit. or cresc. or dim.)

Ossia ; or, or else (at an alternative passage, written in small notes, when a voice part may be too high or too low for anyone but an exceptional singer, or when a time-pattern has to be adjusted to fit the words of a translation).

Pizzicato ; plucked with the finger. (A direction for string players. The word *arco* after a pizzicato passage indicates that the bow is to be used again.)

Poco ; a little. *Poco a poco* ; little by little.

Quasi ; as if (e.g. *quasi recitativo*—like a recitative).

Sempre ; always.

Senza ; without (e.g. *senza rep.*—without repeats, or *senza sord.*—without the mute, *senza vibrato*—without a warm, pulsating tone).

Simile ; in the same way. (This useful word applies to a passage where every note has a sign such as an accent or a staccato dash over it : the sign need only be written over the first few notes, if it is followed by *sim.*)

Subito ; immediately, in the sense of ' unexpectedly ' (e.g. *subito p* after a long crescendo).

SOME SPECIAL SIGNS USED IN INSTRUMENTAL MUSIC.

The sign ⊓ means a down-bow ; the sign ⋁ is for an up-bow.

The sign o above a note indicates a harmonic, one of the

faint overtones in the harmonic series which can be produced on a stringed instrument by lightly touching the string at a certain point in its length. (These points are called NODES : they occur where there is least amplitude in the vibrating string, and they divide it into segments of $\frac{1}{2}$, $\frac{1}{3}$, $\frac{1}{4}$, $\frac{1}{5}$ etc.)

A figure written above a group of notes shows that, as in the triplet, an unusual number of notes is to be played in the duration of the beat.   For example :

The sign for a glissando is an oblique line joining the notes at the beginning and end of the swift journey. (The line is often wavy.)

Harp

Glissandos are played on instruments such as the harp or piano, where they can pass through actual notes in their swift journey up or down.   A slide on a string instrument or a voice passes through microtones : it is described as a PORTAMENTO.

A vertical wavy line before a chord in harp or keyboard music shows that the notes of the chord are to be played one after another, from the lowest to the highest. This is called ARPEGGIANDO. (On the rare occasions when an arpeggiando chord is to be played from the highest note to the lowest, an arrow pointing downwards is written at the bottom of the wavy line.)

COLL' 8VE, written above the high notes or beneath the low notes of a harp or keyboard part, shows that the notes are to be played in octaves.

The abbreviation ⅙ is sometimes used to show that the notes of the previous bar are to be repeated :

A repetition of the same figure within a bar can be shown with the sign ╱ or ╱╱ .

These abbreviations are only meant for use in orchestral scores and parts : they are never found in piano music. Abbreviations for repeated notes, however, can be used in any written or printed part :

Tremolando abbreviations are frequently used for all instrumental parts, including the piano :

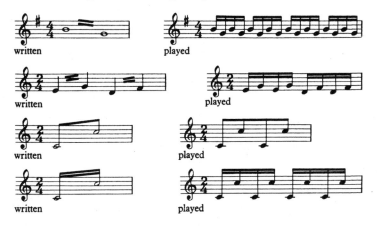

(In music for stringed instruments the word TREMOLO can apply to the rapid repetition of the same note by moving the bow very quickly to and fro, as well as to rapidly alternating notes, which are described as ' fingered tremolo '.)

A ROLL on the timpani, which is a repeated-note tremolando, is indicated with a *tr*⸺⸺ .   This inaccurate sign dates from the seventeenth century, when the two timpani were always tuned to the tonic and dominant.   Composers still use this sign for a roll, in spite of the fact that a genuine trill on two different notes could quite possibly be needed in the changed conditions of twentieth-century music.

Part XIII.   The Twentieth-Century break with Tradition

CHAPTER 54

GETTING AWAY FROM KEY

THE composers who were writing at the beginning of the twentieth century were faced with a problem.   Wagner's chromatic sequences and ' wandering ' chords had apparently stretched the normal diatonic scale to the very limits of its endurance.   His immediate successors began to feel dissatisfied with the old system of keys and key relationships.   This meant that they had to find other intervals than the related notes of the major or minor scale for the raw material of their music.

Many experiments were tried.   The interval of the tritone was used as a pivot, either melodically, moving through whole tones from C up to F♯, or harmonically, moving from the triad of C to the unrelated triad of F♯.   Composers borrowed the modal scales of various national folk songs, including the so-called ' gypsy scale ' with two augmented seconds, C D♭ E F G A♭ B C.   There were several composers who experimented in microtones, using QUARTER-TONES and SIXTH-TONES as melodic intervals.   Others wrote their melodic parts with two different key-signatures (BITONALITY), or with several different key-signatures (POLYTONALITY).

The word TONALITY means ' allegiance to a TONAL CENTRE ' (i.e., the tonic of a mode, as well as the key-note of a key).

During the first quarter of the twentieth century there were composers who felt that it was not enough to get rid of major and minor keys : they also wanted to get rid of tonality.   This led to ATONALITY, where no individual note could have power over any other note—which is as though a verb were to lose its power over the nouns in a sentence of words.   The result, for a while, was chaos.

There were two ways out of the chaos, and both of them are still being followed.   One way was to keep to tonality in its widest sense and to give it new life.   This way has made it possible for ' ordinary ' listeners to enjoy hearing some of the greatest works that have been written in our own time.   It has also made it possible for beginners and amateurs to be given twentieth-century music to sing and play, instead of having to rely entirely on the masterpieces of previous centuries.

The other way out of the chaos of atonality was to follow the entirely new system called the TWELVE-NOTE METHOD OF COMPOSITION.

CHAPTER 55

TWELVE-NOTE SERIAL MUSIC

THE method of composing with ' twelve notes related only to one another ' was evolved in the early nineteen-twenties as a result of experiments made by the Austrian composer Arnold Schoenberg.

The system is founded on the division of the octave into twelve notes a semitone apart, each note being of equal importance.   The notes are not used as degrees of a chromatic scale : they are arranged in a fixed order such as :

$$e♮ \quad e♭' \quad c♯''' \quad c♮'' \quad f♯'' \quad g♮' \quad f♮'' \quad b♭ \quad a♮'' \quad b♭' \quad g♯'' \quad d♮'$$
$$1 \quad 2 \quad 3 \quad 4 \quad 5 \quad 6 \quad 7 \quad 8 \quad 9 \quad 10 \quad 11 \quad 12$$

Any order of the twelve equal-tempered notes can be chosen for a NOTE ROW (or SERIES) to form the basis of an entire SERIAL composition. The row is used forwards, backwards (retrograde), upside-down (inverted) and retrograde-inverted ; and it can be transposed to any other level of pitch. It can be divided up contrapuntally between different instruments or voices, as long as the actual order of the notes keeps strictly to the series. And it can be used vertically to form chords. These chords are not constructed like triads : their intervals are determined by the note-order in the row. They may consist of any combination of from three to twelve notes. But chord-structures in twelve-note music do not produce cadences or other harmonic progressions as in tonal music, because there is no relationship to a key-note.

The word SERIAL is sometimes used as an alternative name for twelve-note music, but this can be confusing as it is possible to borrow the technique of serial composition while using fewer than twelve notes for the note-row (or ' tone-row ' as it is called in America). Serial compositions which use all the twelve notes, as in Schoenberg's method, are more accurately described as TWELVE-NOTE SERIAL MUSIC.

Some of the composers who have followed Schoenberg have aimed at TOTAL SERIALIZATION. This means that not only the notes but also the rhythm and dynamics are controlled by ' serial ' organization. Time-values are arranged in a fixed order, and the dynamics are distributed in strict rotation.

There is nothing new about keeping strictly to the same note-order, whether retrograde or inverted, throughout the whole of a composition. Bach was doing this in the early eighteenth century. And there is nothing new about keeping to a serial order of rhythmical patterns : the great English composer Dunstable was doing this in the early fifteenth century. But Dunstable was using plainsong tunes that every-one knew by heart, so his listeners were able to follow him.

Twentieth-century serial composers know their own note-rows by heart, but the ' ordinary ' listener finds it quite impossible to follow a series at first hearing.   Even the performers sometimes find it difficult to keep their places, particularly in a recent development known as ' serial density ', in which no instrument plays more than a single note at any one entry. It is not surprising that some of the composers of totally serial music have been tempted to plan their works for electronic performance.

CHAPTER 56

ELECTRONIC DEVICES

ELECTRONIC INSTRUMENTS do away with the need for violins and cellos and flutes and horns and drums, for their sound vibrations are produced by electronic impulses.   And ELECTRONIC MUSIC does away with the need for human beings as performers, for it is controlled by the turning of a knob.

Electronic music is a direct result of the mechanical reproduction of music.   The earliest experimental by-product of recording and broadcasting was known as MUSIQUE CONCRÈTE. Sounds, whether human, animal, vegetable, or mineral, were recorded on tape, and amplified, slowed down, quickened, reversed, and superimposed until they were transformed into a series of noises that had never been heard before.

The distorted mixture of overtones and differentials and other combined frequencies used in electronic music produces sounds that are very much stranger than the ' old-fashioned ' *musique concrète* of the early nineteen-fifties.   Electronic music cannot be written down in musical notation, for its ' score ' is a graph of frequency ratios and decibel numbers. It has ' complexes ' instead of notes, and its nearest approach to a chord is a ' complex of complexes '. Its highest audible compass can sound more grotesque than the rapid unwinding of a tape-recorder, and its range of dynamics can make a listener feel giddy. As an experiment in applied acoustics it has fascinating possibilities, for it can follow the disciplined order of a logical design. But it has no use for human performers, whether professional or amateur. And it has nothing to offer the learner who wants some music to sing or play.

CODA

If electronic devices were to have the last word it would make a gloomy ending to a book written for learners and amateur music-makers.

It is true that musical life is at present going through what is known as ' a state of crisis '. The alluring possibilities of electronic sounds are leading some of the keenest young composers further and further away from the live performance of music. And the gap between serial music and tonal music is growing wider and wider. But music itself has survived many crises in the past, and so-called ' transitional ' periods have produced some of the greatest geniuses.

In spite of the crisis, the learners of today are far better off than they would have been fifty years ago. To begin with, there is the immense wealth of great music waiting to be heard every week. Without stirring from their homes, learners can listen to the symphonies of Schubert and the string quartets of Mozart ; to the Passion music of Bach and the earliest experiments in Italian opera ; to the consort music that Shakespeare heard when he went out to dinner and the medieval motets that were being sung in English cathedrals when Chaucer was writing his *Canterbury Tales*.

Listening to a record or to a broadcast performance can be an overwhelming musical experience, but we have to remember, while counting our blessings, that we are losing a great deal that matters. We lose the give and take between performer and audience which is one of the essential ingredients in listening. And when we hear the same record over and over again we lose the uniqueness of the performance. Music is not meant to be fixed and unalterable : it has to be newly brought to life each time it is sung or played. For this reason amateur singers and players are often better than record-listeners at understanding what music is about, even though they may not always be able to keep in tune or in time.

During the last twenty years there has been a tremendous increase in the amount of help given to amateur music-making. Today it is true to say that anyone who is prepared for a great deal of hard work has a chance of joining an amateur choir or orchestra or string class or recorder group. And fortunately there is enough singable and playable music to last for a life-time.

Not only are there folk songs and medieval carols and sixteenth-century madrigals and seventeenth-century dances waiting for beginners to learn their notes on ; there are also exciting contemporary works being written specially for amateurs. Benjamin Britten's *Noye's Fludde* has orchestral parts for descant recorders, ' open-string ' violins, bugles from a boys' school, hand-bells from a youth club, and home-made percussion instruments, including a row of china mugs strung on a length of string and hit with a wooden spoon.

There can be no doubt that the second half of the twentieth century is an encouraging time for the beginner who is still learning the musical alphabet.

Index of Terms

In this list of terms, only the page-number on which the actual definition occurs is mentioned. The approximate pronunciation of some of the less familiar foreign terms, shown in brackets, is taken from Percy Scholes's *Oxford Companion to Music* (O.U.P.).

OXFORD

MORE OXFORD PAPERBACKS

This book is just one of nearly 1000 Oxford Paperbacks currently in print. If you would like details of other Oxford Paperbacks, including titles in the World's Classics, Oxford Reference, Oxford Books, OPUS, Past Masters, Oxford Authors, and Oxford Shakespeare series, please write to:

UK and Europe: Oxford Paperbacks Publicity Manager, Arts and Reference Publicity Department, Oxford University Press, Walton Street, Oxford OX2 6DP.

Customers in UK and Europe will find Oxford Paperbacks available in all good bookshops. But in case of difficulty please send orders to the Cash-with-Order Department, Oxford University Press Distribution Services, Saxon Way West, Corby, Northants NN18 9ES. Tel: 01536 741519; Fax: 01536 746337. Please send a cheque for the total cost of the books, plus £1.75 postage and packing for orders under £20; £2.75 for orders over £20. Customers outside the UK should add 10% of the cost of the books for postage and packing.

USA: Oxford Paperbacks Marketing Manager, Oxford University Press, Inc., 200 Madison Avenue, New York, N.Y. 10016.

Canada: Trade Department, Oxford University Press, 70 Wynford Drive, Don Mills, Ontario M3C 1J9.

Australia: Trade Marketing Manager, Oxford University Press, G.P.O. Box 2784Y, Melbourne 3001, Victoria.

South Africa: Oxford University Press, P.O. Box 1141, Cape Town 8000.

Oxford
Paperback
Reference

OXFORD PAPERBACK REFERENCE

From *Art and Artists* to *Zoology*, the Oxford Paperback Reference series offers the very best subject reference books at the most affordable prices.

Authoritative, accessible, and up to date, the series features dictionaries in key student areas, as well as a range of fascinating books for a general readership. Included are such well-established titles as Fowler's *Modern English Usage*, Margaret Drabble's *Concise Companion to English Literature*, and the bestselling science and medical dictionaries.

The series has now been relaunched in handsome new covers. Highlights include new editions of some of the most popular titles, as well as brand new paperback reference books on *Politics*, *Philosophy*, and *Twentieth-Century Poetry*.

With new titles being constantly added, and existing titles regularly updated, Oxford Paperback Reference is unrivalled in its breadth of coverage and expansive publishing programme. New dictionaries of *Film*, *Economics*, *Linguistics*, *Architecture*, *Archaeology*, *Astronomy*, and *The Bible* are just a few of those coming in the future.